D0234654

BEST OF

Paris

Rob Flynn

contents

Paris Condensed reprinted as
Best of Paris – March 2004
2nd edition – February 2002
First published – April 2000

Published by
Lonely Planet Publications Pty Ltd
ABN 36 005 607 983
90 Maribyrnong St, Footscray, Vic 3011, Australia
www.lonelyplanet.com or AOL keyword: lp

Lonely Planet offices
Australia Locked Bag 1, Footscray, Vic 3011
☎ 613 8379 8000 fax 613 8379 8111
e talk2us@lonelyplanet.com.au
USA   150 Linden St, Oakland, CA 94607
☎ 510 893 8555 Toll Free: 800 275 8555
fax 510 893 8572
e info@lonelyplanet.com
UK   10a Spring Place, London NW5 3BH
☎ 020 7428 4800 fax 020 7428 4828
e go@lonelyplanet.co.uk
France 1 rue du Dahomey, 75011 Paris
☎ 01 55 25 33 00 fax 01 55 25 33 01
e bip@lonelyplanet.fr
www.lonelyplanet.fr

Maps Charles Rawlings-Way Design James Hardy
Editing Miriam Cannell & Gabrielle Green Publishing
Managers Diana Saad & Katrina Browning Thanks to
Annie Horner, Brett Pascoe, Gerard Walker, Jane Hart,
Lachlan Ross, Nikki Anderson, Rowan McKinnon, Soph'
Rivoire and Tim Ryder.

Photographs
Many of the images in this guide are available for
licensing from Lonely Planet Images.
e lpi@lonelyplanet.com.au;
www.lonelyplanetimages.com
Images also used with kind permission of Bridgeman
Art Library, London.

Front cover photograph
The Louvre
(Richard l'Anson)

ISBN 1 74104 439 1

Text & maps © Lonely Planet Publications 2002
Transit map © RATP - CML Agence Cartographique
Photos © photographers as indicated 2002
Printed by The Bookmaker International Ltd,
Printed in China

how to use this book

SYMBOLS

- ✉ address
- ☎ telephone number
- **e** email/website address
- **Ⓜ** nearest metro station
- **Ⓡ** nearest train station
- 🚌 nearest bus route
- ◷ opening hours
- ⓘ tourist information
- ⑨ cost, entry charge
- ♿ wheelchair access
- ⚲ child-friendly
- ✕ on-site or nearby eatery
- **V** good vegetarian selection

COLOUR-CODING

Each chapter has a different colour code which is reflected on the maps for quick reference (eg all Highlights are bright yellow on the maps).

MAPS

The fold-out maps inside front and back covers are numbered from 1 to 5. All sights and venues in the text have map references which indicate where to find them on the maps; eg (3, G12) means Map 3, grid reference 12. Although each item is not pin-pointed on the maps, the street address is always indicated.

PRICES

Price gradings (eg €10/5/30) usually indicate adult/concession/family entry charges to a venue. All prices in this book are quoted in euros (€); see Money on page 113 for details.

AUTHOR AUTHOR !

Rob Flynn

On the eve of the last millennium Sydney-born Rob headed up to the city of lights, where he settled on the edge of the Marais.

When he's not looking for the perfect cafe terrace or the best Margaux by-the-glass in Paris (all in the cause of making this a better guide, of course!), Rob is the head of Lonely Planet's New Media unit responsible for Lonely Planet's websites, digital travel guides and other arcane stuff.

Thanks to Annabel for the calls & clubs and Arno for the bars. *Merci infiniment à mes copains de Lonely Planet France - je vous embrasse tous.* Special thanks to St Germain, David Gray, Maggie Jones, Leopold Fucker, and the blue-eyed angel atop La Tour Eiffel for keeping me sane and happy in the wee small hours.

READER FEEDBACK

Things change – prices go up, schedules change, good places go bad and bad places improve or go bankrupt. So, if you find things better or worse, recently opened or long since closed, please tell us and help make the next edition even more accurate. Send all correspondence to the Lonely Planet office closest to you (listed on p. 2) or visit www.lonelyplanet.com/feedback.

facts about paris

Paris is the most seductive city on the planet, with beauty, art and romance in spades. But, to the unfamiliar, it can also seem intimidating. It's not just the acres of museums and wall-to-wall art, culture and *haute couture* – it's the horror stories of cramped hotel rooms, rip-off prices and rude locals.

But Paris has changed. No longer the living museum or Gallic theme park it may have seemed a generation ago, it's now a welcoming, fun and increasingly cosmopolitan city.

Parisians believe they have *savoir-faire* – the art of knowing how to live well – and indeed you'll find that Paris is a sensory feast. It's a city to gaze at, with its wide boulevards, impressive monuments, great works of art and magic lights. It's a city to savour, with its great cheese, chocolate, wine and seafood. It's a city to listen to, whether you crave opera, jazz or techno. It's a city to smell: the perfume boutiques, fresh coffee and croissants, chestnuts roasting in winter. It's a city to feel: the wind in your face as you rollerblade through Bastille or cycle along the Seine, or the *frisson* of fear and pleasure as you peer out from atop the Tour Eiffel.

Above all, it's a city to discover. So do the sites, visit the museums – they're part of the experience. But then jump on the metro or a bus and get off at a place you've never heard of, wander through a *quartier* where French mixes with Arabic or Vietnamese, poke your head into mysterious shops, have lunch in a local restaurant, or just perch on a cafe terrace with a *vin blanc* and let yourself fall in love with your very own Paris.

Mis en Seine – a cruise boat passes under the Pont des Arts

HISTORY
The Gauls & the Romans
The Île de la Cité was settled during the 3rd century BC by a tribe of Celtic Gaul river-traders known as the Parisii. Centuries of conflict between the Gauls and Rome ended in 52BC, when Julius Caesar's legions took control of the territory and established the Roman town of Lutetia on the island and the left (south) bank of the Seine.

In AD508, the Frankish king Clovis I united Gaul as a kingdom and made Paris (as the town was now known) his capital. Despite a succession of raids by the Scandinavian Vikings during the 9th century, Paris soon prospered as the capital of the kingdom of Francia and a centre of politics, commerce, religion and culture.

The Middle Ages
In the 12th century, construction began on the greatest creation of medieval Paris, the cathedral of Notre Dame (completed nearly 200 years later). The Marais (marsh) area north of the Seine was drained and the Right Bank developed as the town's mercantile centre. The food markets at Les Halles opened in 1110, and the Louvre was built as a riverside fortress around 1200. Meanwhile, the south bank of the Seine developed as a place of scholarship and learning (hence 'Latin' quarter), the Sorbonne opening its doors in 1253.

The Renaissance
Paris eagerly embraced the culture of the Italian Renaissance in the early 16th century, and many of the city's signature buildings and monuments were built during the period, including the Pont Neuf, the Église St-Eustache and the Hôtel (now Musée) Carnavalet.

My Kingdom for a Mass
When Paris' new Protestant king took the throne as Henri IV in 1589, the ultra-Catholic Parisians refused him entry to the city, and a five year siege of the capital ensued. Only when he embraced Catholicism did the capital relent. *Paris vaut bien une messe* (Paris is well worth a Mass), he is reputed to have said upon taking communion.

Henri IV (ruled 1589-1610) rebuilt Paris in grand style, including the magnificent Place Royal (now the Place des Vosges) and Place Dauphine.

Louis XIV & the Ancien Régime
Louis XIV, known as le Roi Soleil (the Sun King), ascended to the throne in 1643 at the tender age of five and held the Crown until 1715. During his reign he nearly bankrupted the national treasury with prolonged bouts of battling and building. His most tangible legacy is the palace at Versailles, 23km south-west of Paris, but he also commissioned the fine Place Vendôme, Place des Victoires, Invalides and the Louvre's Cour Carrée.

A century later, the excesses of Louis XVI and his capricious queen, Marie-Antoinette, led to an uprising of Parisians and, on 14 July 1789, the storming of the Bastille prison, the ultimate symbol of the despotism of the *ancien régime*. The French Revolution had begun.

Revolution & Napoleon

The moderate populist ideals of the Revolution's early stages quickly gave way to the Reign of Terror; over 17,000 people were introduced to *madame la guillotine,* including Louis XVI and his queen, and eventually many of the original 'patriots' such as Robespierre.

The Unkindest Cut

Dr Guillotine used sheep to perfect his 'philanthropic decapitating machine', before it was adopted as the Terror's chief persuader. Surprisingly, the guillotine was used by the state until September 1977.

The unstable post-Revolution government was consolidated in 1799 under a young Corsican general, Napoleon Bonaparte, who crowned himself 'Emperor of the French' at Notre Dame in 1804, and proceeded to sweep most of Europe under his wing. The Arc de Triomphe and the Code Napoléon (still the basis of the French legal system) are among his legacies.

The Second Empire

Following Napoleon's defeat at Waterloo and subsequent exile to St Helena in 1815, France faltered under a string of mostly inept rulers until a coup d'état in 1851 ushered in the Second Empire and a new emperor, Napoleon III (nephew of Bonaparte). Napoleon III charged Baron Haussmann with the task of demolishing the old, cramped, dark and insanitary city in order to rebuild Paris as a great imperial capital. Over the next 18 years Haussmann transformed Paris into the city we recognise today, with its wide boulevards, fine public buildings (the Garnier Opera House being the jewel in the crown) and sculptured parks.

Inevitably, Napoleon III's pugnacity led to a costly and unsuccessful war with the Prussians in 1870. The Emperor was captured and Parisians took to the streets, demanding that a republic be declared. A battle for power ensued between supporters of the monarchist government and the republicans of the Paris Commune, who briefly took over Paris. Some 20,000 Communards were summarily executed during the insurrection.

La Marseillaise, Arc de Triomphe

Rachel Imeson

The Belle Époque to the Present

Despite its bloody beginnings, the Third Republic ushered in the glittering *belle époque* (beautiful age), with its famed Art Nouveau architecture and a barrage of advances in the arts and sciences. The Tour Eiffel, Impressionism and the Paris of nightclubs and artistic cafes are legacies of this time. By the 1920s and 30s, Paris had become a worldwide centre for the artistic and intellectual avant-garde.

The exuberance of the period was snuffed out by the Nazi occupation of Paris – Hitler strode beneath the Arc de Triomphe in June 1940. Thousands of Jews living in Paris were sent to Nazi concentration and extermination camps, while the Resistance operated from subterranean headquarters in the Catacombes. In August 1944, a bitter Hitler ordered his retreating army to raze the city; thankfully, his general refused.

Sound Memory

At noon on the first Wednesday of each month, air-raid sirens are tested throughout Paris – a chilling reminder that this has not always been a peaceful, serene city.

After the war, Paris regained its position as a creative hotbed and nurtured a revitalised liberalism that reached its crescendo in the student-led 'Spring Uprising' of 1968, when some nine million people joined in a paralysing general strike sparked by opposition to the De Gaulle government and the Vietnam War.

Gauche or gorgeous? The girdle-like Grande Arche de La Défense

During the 1980s, President François Mitterrand initiated his visionary *grands travaux*, a series of ambitious building projects designed to transform the face of Paris. Responses to the most provocative designs, such as the Musée du Louvre's glass pyramid and the Grande Arche de La Défense, range from appalled to rapturous.

In July 1998, a million ecstatic Parisians choked the Champs Élysées following France's first-ever World Cup football victory. The against-the-odds win (3-0 over Brazil) by a mixed-race team was trumpeted as a symbolic achievement of a newly self-confident, vigorous and pluralistic France – a sentiment reinforced by the election in 2001 of Paris' first leftist (and openly gay) mayor in 150 years.

ORIENTATION

Paris is a remarkably compact city (around 10km in diameter), built on the banks of the river Seine in the central north of France. The perimeter of the city is roughly defined by the blvd Périphérique, the ring road which separates the city from the *banlieus* (suburbs).

Conventionally, the Seine divides the well-heeled Right Bank (Rive Droite), north of the river, from the more bohemian Left Bank (Rive Gauche) – though today the social division is more between the bourgeois and right-leaning west and the younger, socialist-voting east. On the Right Bank are the Louvre, the Champs Élysées, the Marais and the most exclusive shopping districts; on the Left Bank, the Quartier Latin, the Musée d'Orsay and blvds St-Michel and St-Germain.

Paris is divided into 20 numbered *arrondissements* (districts) that spiral clockwise from the city centre like a conch shell. While some Parisian *quartiers* have names, most addresses simply refer to the arrondissement (in this guide we follow local usage: 1er, 2e, 3e etc). The Tour Eiffel dominates the western end of the city, Montparnasse tower the south and Sacré Cœur the north, while Bastille is a prominent landmark in the east.

ENVIRONMENT

For a densely populated, inland, urban centre, inhabited for more than two millennia, Paris is a surprisingly clean and healthy city. Thanks are due mainly to Baron Haussmann, who radically reshaped the city in the second half of the 19th century, widening streets, building parks, and modernising the sewer and storm-water systems.

Despite the city's excellent public transport system, Haussmann's wide boulevards are usually choked with traffic, and air pollution is the city's major environmental hazard. Car owners are encouraged to leave their vehicles at home or drive more slowly on high pollution days. Second on the list is probably the noise generated by the same traffic – especially motorbikes and trucks (a pair of earplugs is a worthwhile investment for a sound night's sleep).

Poochy le Pew

Each year more than 600 people are admitted to hospital after slipping on dog shit in Paris streets, and thousands more have unpleasant minor catastrophes. The government prefers to spend some €1.5 million annually on cleaning up after dogs (most visibly the two-wheeled *moto-crottes*) rather than tackle changing the attitudes and practices of dog-owners.

It went that a way, inspector.

Indoors, be prepared to inhale second-hand cigarette (and even cigar) smoke pretty much everywhere – including in restaurants and nonsmoking areas.

Fortunately, Parisians are rediscovering the *vélo* (bicycle), and a network of some 130km of city bicycle lanes has been created over the past few years.

GOVERNMENT & POLITICS

Parisians love politics. Which is just as well, because there's no lack of politicians. Paris is home to the French president (Jacques Chirac), the prime minister (Lionel Jospin) and his government, the National Assembly, the Senate, the *maire* (mayor) of Paris (Bertrand Delanoe), the mayor's 18 *adjoints* (deputy mayors), the 163 members of the Conseil de Paris (Council of Paris), the mayors of each of the 20 *arrondissements* (plus their councils) and local European Parliament members.

Political debate is dominated by the right/left (*droite/gauche*), conservative/socialist divide, and there's a revolving door of personalities; Chirac, for instance, was mayor of Paris (the first actually elected since the Revolution) and prime minister before being elected president.

Parisian politics has always had a radical edge (ask Louis XVI), and it's not uncommon to hear nostalgic references to 1968, the year that violent student protests in Paris and general strikes brought down the De Gaulle government. Police in riot gear are still bussed in to 'control' the almost weekly peaceful *manifestations* (demonstrations) which rally at Bastille or République.

ECONOMY

Paris is a major European capital, home to the European headquarters of many multinational companies, and also the heart of France's own commercial, industrial and financial sectors: about 20% of all economic activity in France takes place in the Paris region. A highly centralised bureaucracy means the capital also accounts for around 40% of the nation's white-collar jobs. Paris has also become a multimedia centre, with thriving telecommunications, digital arts and Internet industries.

After many years of sluggish growth and double-digit unemployment, the French economy has recently enjoyed good times, with unemployment falling to 8.5%, just above the euro zone average.

The city itself is predominantly middle-class, most of the workers having been pushed into the suburbs by rising rents. There are estimated to be more than 50,000 *sans-abri* (homeless) on the streets of Paris; beggars exist but are not common.

Did You Know?

- Paris is the world's No.1 tourist destination: more than 26 million people visited Paris in 2000, 60% from other countries.
- Average salaries range between €1500 and €5000 per month.
- Employers pay an additional 40% of this amount into the French social security system, which covers unemployment benefits, health care and retirement pensions.
- Monthly apartment rentals average around €15 per sq m (an 80-sq-m 2-bedroom apartment costs around €1250 per month).

John Hay

Legions lurve le Louvre.

SOCIETY & CULTURE

The population of Paris is about 2.2 million, while the Île de France (the greater metropolitan area of Paris) has about 10 million inhabitants – about 17% of France's total population of 58 million people. Paris today is a very cosmopolitan city, with many residents from other nations of the EU and a large English-speaking population.

In the second half of the 20th century France experienced waves of immigration, particularly from former French colonies in North Africa and French-speaking sub-Saharan Africa. During the late 1950s and early 60s, over a million French settlers returned to metro-politan France from Algeria, other parts of Africa and Indochina.

The French are generally more relaxed about relations between men and women – and about sex – than visitors might be accustomed to. Paris has thriving gay and les-bian communities, and same-sex couples are a common sight on its streets. Pigalle and rue St Denis

Masses mix it on the Metro.

are the best known red light areas; prostitution, though illegal, is tolerat-ed and openly touted by streetwalkers in certain quarters of the city.

Etiquette

While the stereotype of the haughty, arrogant and unhelpful Parisian may have been accurate 20 years ago it's certainly not true today. Parisians tend to be shy with strangers, but will readily help if approached in a friendly manner and with a word or two of attempted French.

Some Useful Dos and Don'ts Include:

- Always say 'Bonjour' when you walk into a shop, and 'Merci, monsieur/madame/mademoiselle ... au revoir' when you leave.
- If you want help or to interrupt someone, begin with 'Excusez-moi, mon-sieur/madame/mademoiselle'.
- People who know each other usually exchange *bises* (kisses) as a greeting (including men if they are close friends). The usual ritual is one glancing peck on each cheek. People who don't kiss each other will almost always shake hands.
- In a restaurant, summon the waiter by saying 's'il vous plaît' (please), not 'garçon', which means 'boy' and is considered rude.
- Take flowers (not chrysanthemums – they're only for funerals) or a bottle of wine if you are invited to someone's home to visit.

ARTS

A century ago Paris held centre stage in the art world, attracting many of the painters, writers and musicians who forged the modern period. Paris has retained this reputation thanks in part to the city's peerless architectural beauty – evident in the ground-breaking Gothic Notre Dame, ostentatiously Baroque Palais du Luxembourg, seriously classical Panthéon and Arc de Triomphe, and the Art Nouveau detailing on everything from metro entrances to bistros.

Literature & Music

The country's literary legacy is equally statuesque, from Molière, Racine, Voltaire and Rousseau to Hugo, Balzac, Zola, Proust, de Beauvoir and Camus.

The 19th century saw the rise of a number of musical luminaries such as Hector Berlioz, César

Thumbs up for Parisian art, Parvis Garden of Contemporary Art (p. 18)

Franck, George Bizet, Claude Debussy and Maurice Ravel. But it hasn't all been high culture: jazz hit Paris with a bang in the 1920s, producing violinist Stéphane Grappelli and legendary Romany guitarist Django Reinhardt, while popular singers who made an impact include Edith Piaf, Jacques Brel and Serge Gainsbourg.

Today French musicians are back at the cutting edge through internationally known electronic music groups like Air, Daft Punk and Cassius, and through DJs such as Laurent Garnier and Bob Sinclar.

Foreign Writers in Paris

Much of our fascination with Paris can be traced to the English-speaking writers who found inspiration here, beginning with Charles Dickens' *A Tale of Two Cities*. Hemingway's *A Moveable Feast* portrays bohemian life in Paris, and Gertrude Stein's *The Autobiography of Alice B Toklas* is a fascinating account of the author's many years in Paris and her friendships with Matisse, Picasso, Braque, Hemingway and others. George Orwell's *Down and Out in Paris and London* includes an account of his time as a penniless dishwasher in Paris. Both *Tropic of Cancer* and *Tropic of Capricorn* by Henry Miller are steamy autobiographical novels set in the French capital, published in France in the 1930s but banned in the UK and USA until the 1960s.

Cinema

France's place in film history was assured when the Lumière brothers invented 'moving pictures'; directors René Clair, Marcel Carné and Jean Renoir invented avant-garde cinema; Jean-Luc Godard, François Truffaut and Alain Resnais invented *nouvelle vague*; Jacques Tati invented Monsieur Hulot; and actors Anna Karina (*Alphaville*) and Jean-Paul Belmondo (*À Bout de Souffle*/Breathless) invented Parisian cool.

French cinema is still going strong – exporting actors like Gerard Depardieu, Catherine Deneuve, Juliette Binoche, Daniel Auteuil, Virginie Ledoyen and Sophie Marceau, and with popular international successes like Jean-Pierre Jeunet's 2001 *Le Fabuleux Destin d'Amélie Poulain* (Amélie from Montmartre).

Painting

However, it's in the world of oils and watercolours that Paris has truly inspired. According to Voltaire it began with Nicolas Poussin (1594-1665) and Claude Lorrain (1600-82), painters of eerily light-drenched classical scenes. The neoclassical and Romantic movements rejected pastel hues, with David and Géricault painting enough house-sized historical scenes to (almost) fill the Louvre.

Pastoral themes returned with the Barbizon School of Corot and Millet, who gathered to paint in the open air (at that time a novel concept), and the idea really took off with the headline-grabbing Impressionists, led by Claude Monet. Innovative artists inspired by the idea of capturing the fleeting effects of light included Sisley, Seurat, Pisarro, Renoir, Degas, Toulouse-Lautrec, Cézanne, Gauguin and Rousseau. Ensuing movements such as Symbolism (Moreau), Fauvism (Matisse and Derain), Cubism (Picasso and Braque) and Dadaism (Duchamp) ensured that Paris' cafes, studios and attics were filled with artists, both French and foreign-born. In the 21st century, the city continues to be a spiritual home for artists, aesthetes and romantics alike.

Rob Flynn

Pavement or palais: Paris is a painter's perfect canvas and a paradise for art lovers of every persuasion.

highlights

Paris, like traditional French cuisine, has a surfeit of riches. Many visitors make the mistake of trying to taste everything in too short a time – the Louvre, the Tour Eiffel, the Centre Pompidou, Sacré Cœur, blvd St-Germain, the Arc de Triomphe – ending up with severe indigestion.

It's impossible to see everything that Paris has to offer on a short visit – so don't even try. Make sure you see the few sights you're really passionate about, and then just get out there and explore.

Paris sees more tourists than just about any other city on earth, which means there'll be queues and crowds at all of the top attractions. If you plan to tackle the major sites, the best strategy is to start early, pace yourself, and make sure you take a good book or fascinating companion to keep you occupied while queuing. Late in the day is also a good time to visit sites, but keep in mind that ticket sales usually stop 15-45mins before closing time.

Finally, don't miss seeing Paris by night. The river and monuments are transformed after dark, and even the traffic seems to add to the magic when viewed from afar.

Place des Vosges

Stopping Over?

One Day Start with a stroll around the Île de la Cité and Île St-Louis, not forgetting to pay your respects to Notre Dame; lunch on the terrace of La Samaritaine department store overlooking the Seine; head down to the Tour Eiffel for the view at dusk; cruise back up the river by boat before having dinner and a nightcap in the Marais.

Two Days Spend the morning at the Louvre or the Musée d'Orsay, according to taste; after a picnic lunch in the Square du Vert Galant, take an afternoon stroll around Montmartre and make a night of it at the restaurants and bars around Bastille or rue Oberkampf.

Paris Lowlights

Bastille Paris' most famous monument that doesn't exist – the prison site is now a busy traffic roundabout.

Boulevard St-Michel Avoid the rip-off cafes and fast-food joints.

Les Halles Probably the world's ugliest and most confusing shopping mall.

Three Days Shop! Head for the department stores near Opéra, browse the backstreets of the Marais or St-Germain, or raid the designer boutiques of rue St-Honoré and Place des Victoires. Visit a small museum – perhaps the Rodin or Cluny – and dine at the most expensive traditional French restaurant you can afford.

ARC DE TRIOMPHE & CHAMPS ÉLYSÉES (3, B2)

Napoleon's Arc de Triomphe towers 50m above Place Charles de Gaulle (or Place d'Étoile – 'Star Place'), the vast traffic roundabout from which 12 grand boulevards radiate. From the top of the arch (284 steps, and well worth the effort) you can look straight down the greatest of these boulevards, av des Champs Élysées, to the Place de la Concorde.

The arch was commissioned by Napoleon in 1806 to commemorate his great battle victories, but was still under construction when he met his Waterloo in 1815; it was finally completed in 1836. The best known of the four high-relief panels (on the right as you face the arch from the Champs Élysées) is François Rude's *La Marseillaise* (see p. 7).

The 2km-long Champs Élysées was popular with the aristocracy of the mid-19th century as a stage on which to parade their wealth. Since WWII, it has been taken over by airline offices, cinemas, car showrooms and fast-food restaurants.

The wealthy denizens of the exclusive **Triangle d'Or** area next door consider the Champs Élysées to be completely degraded and popularised (by which they mean the same thing). In the last few years beautification works have returned some of the former sparkle and prestige to the avenue.

Richard l'Anson

Triumphant Steps

Among the armies to march triumphantly through the arch and down the Champs Élysées were the Germans in 1871, the Allies in 1919, the Germans again in 1940 and the Allies in 1944. Since 1920, the body of an Unknown Soldier from the WWI battlefield of Verdun has lain beneath the arch.

Martin Moos

One of Napoleon's arch triumphs

CENTRE POMPIDOU   (5, B7)

The Centre Georges Pompidou (also known as the Centre Beaubourg) has amazed and delighted visitors since it was built in the mid-1970s – not just for its outstanding collection of modern art, but for its radical (at the time) architectural statement.

In order to keep the exhibition halls as spacious and uncluttered as possible, the architects – the Italian Renzo Piano and Briton Richard Rogers – put the building's 'insides' on the outside. The purpose of each of the ducts, pipes and vents that enclose the centre's glass walls can be divined from the paint job: escalators and lifts in red, electrical circuitry in yellow, the plumbing green and the air-con system blue. The building reopened on the first day of the new millennium after a two-year refit, with new exhibition spaces – and a new coat of gleaming white paint for the western facade.

The Pompidou attracts more than 25,000 visitors a day, thanks in part to its vigorous schedule of outstanding temporary exhibitions. Two floors are dedicated to exhibiting some of the 40,000-plus works of the **Musée National d'Art Moderne (MNAM)** – France's national collection of 20th-century art – including works by the Fauves, Surrealists and Cubists, pop art and contemporary works.

The **Atelier Brancusi**, the studio of the Romanian-born sculptor Constantin Brancusi (1876-1957), contains almost 140 examples of his work as well as drawings, paintings and glass photographic plates.

The open spaces around the centre – especially **Place Igor Stravinsky** – are filled with modern sculpture, street performers and gawkers, and are as much fun as the centre itself.

INFORMATION

- ✉ rue St-Martin, 4e
- ☎ 01 44 78 12 33
- e www.centre pompidou.fr
- Ⓜ Rambuteau
- 🚌 21, 29, 38, 47, 58, 69, 70, 72, 74, 75, 76, 81, 85, 96
- ⏱ 11am-10pm (closed Tues)
- ⑤ €8.54/6.40/4.57, depending on exhibitions chosen; under 18 free to MNAM; under 13 free to exhibitions
- ♿ OK, access through Atelier Brancusi
- ✕ Georges rooftop restaurant & cafe

Spouting art in and out.

Olivier Cirendini

Neil Setchfield

DON'T MISS
- wacky Fontaine Stravinsky ● view from the roof terrace
- street theatre and buskers

CHÂTEAU DE VERSAILLES (1, C6)

The grandest and most famous château in France was the kingdom's political capital and the seat of the royal court between 1682 and 1789. Despite the crowds and queues (it attracts more than three million visitors a year), it's a fascinating and enjoyable place to spend half a day, or even longer – especially on a fine day when visitors can enjoy the immense gardens.

The enormous château was built in the mid-1600s during the reign of Louis XIV (the Sun King) as a symbol of the absolute power of the French monarchy, wreaking havoc on the kingdom's finances in the process. Its scale and decor reflect Louis XIV's taste for profligate luxury and his near boundless appetite for self-glorification. Some 30,000 workers and soldiers toiled to complete the structure.

The complex consists of four main parts: the palace, a 580m-long building with innumerable wings, grand halls and sumptuous bedchambers; the vast gardens, canals and pools west of the palace; and two smaller palaces – the Grand Trianon and Petit Trianon.

Palace highlights include the dazzling **Galeries des Glaces** (Hall of Mirrors; best in the late afternoon), **Opéra Royal**, the **Chapelle Royale** and the **Grands Appartements**.

Diana Mayfield

INFORMATION

✉ Versailles, 23km from Paris
☎ 01 30 83 78 00
🔘 www.chateau versailles.fr
🚃 RER line C; SNCF from Gare St-Lazare or Gare Montparnasse
🕐 château Tues-Sun 9am-5.30pm (May-Sept to 6.30pm); gardens dawn-dusk
⑤ château €6.90/5.35 (free under 18); Grand/Petit Trianon €5.05/3.05; gardens free, except for concerts (Sun Apr-Oct; Sat Jul-Aug)
ⓘ tourist office ☎ 01 39 50 36 22, 2bis av de Paris, Versailles; tours in English
♿ limited
✕ cafe, La Flottille Restaurant

Let Them Eat Cake

On 5 October 1789, a mob of women protesting about bread shortages marched the 23km from Paris to Versailles. Marie-Antoinette escaped the mob using a secret passage, but the next day, after several of the demonstrators and palace guardsmen had been killed, both Louis XVI and his queen were dragged back to Paris – never to see Versailles again.

The Trianons are situated in the middle of the park, about 1.5km from the palace itself. Nearby is the **Hameau de la Reine** (Queen's Hamlet), a mock village of thatched cottages built for the amusement of Marie-Antoinette.

Each Sunday afternoon (3.30-5pm mid-April to October) the fountains are orchestrated to music for the Grandes Eaux Musicales.

CIMETIÈRE DU PÈRE LACHAISE   (2, E13)

Founded in 1804, Père Lachaise Cemetery is the most visited necropolis in the world. Its 70,000 ornate (and at times ostentatious) tombs of the rich and/or famous form a verdant, open-air sculpture garden.

INFORMATION

- ⊠ blvd de Ménilmontant, 20e
- ☎ 01 40 71 75 60
- Ⓜ Philippe Auguste; Père Lachaise; Gambetta
- 🚌 26, 61, 69
- ⏲ 8am-6pm (Sat from 8.30am, Sun from 9am)
- Ⓢ free; tours €5.65/4.15
- ⓘ tours (in French) Sat 2.30pm (also Tues & Sun)
- ♿ limited

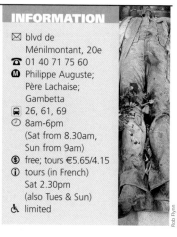

Among the 1 million people buried here are the composer Chopin; the writers Molière, Apollinaire, Oscar Wilde, Balzac, Marcel Proust, Gertrude Stein (and Alice B Toklas) and Colette; artists David, Delacroix, Pisarro, Seurat and Modigliani; actors Sarah Bernhardt, Simone Signoret and Yves Montand; singer Edith Piaf; dancer Isadora Duncan; and even those immortal 12th-century lovers Abélard and Héloïse, the cemetery's oldest residents.

Most young visitors make a bee-line for the Division 6 grave of 1960s rock star **Jim Morrison**, lead singer of the Doors, who died (or did he?) in an apartment on rue Beautreillis in the Marais in 1971.

On 27 May 1871, the last of the Communard insurgents, cornered by government forces, fought a hopeless, all-night battle among the tombstones. In the morning, the 147 survivors were lined up against the **Mur des Fédérés** (Federalists' Wall) and shot. They were buried in a mass grave where they fell.

The cemetery has four entrances, two of them on blvd de Ménilmontant. Maps indicating the location of noteworthy graves are posted around the cemetery and can be obtained free from the Conservation office. Newsstands and kiosks in the area sell the more detailed *Plan Illustré du Père Lachaise* (Illustrated Map of Père Lachaise), which is worth the small asking price if you're interested in exploring for an hour or two.

People are still dying to get into Père Lachaise: the cemetery caters for around 1000 burials and 4000 cremations a year.

Devilish Angels

Oscar Wilde's tomb features a carved angel whose genitals were considered so obscene they are said to have been hacked off and used as a paperweight by the cemetery's director. Meanwhile, those on the effigy of Victor Noir are noticeably intact and are rubbed by wishful-thinking passers-by.

Born to be Wilde; outrageous to the end.

LA DÉFENSE (2, B1)

La Défense is where Paris puts all the buildings that other cities usually put downtown. Here you'll find all the concrete, glass and steel your big-city heart desires – but with a very French twist. Set on the banks of the Seine, just to the west of the 17e *arrondissement*, it puts a radically different perspective on 21st-century Paris.

One of the world's most ambitious urban construction projects, La Défense (named after the monument on the site commemorating the 1871 defence of Paris from the Prussians) was begun in the late 1950s. Some 60 gleaming skyscrapers housing corporate head offices and high-tech government institutions populate the 80-hectare site.

The remarkable **Grande Arche**, surely one of the weirdest buildings on earth, is the biggest drawcard. Designed by Danish architect Otto von Spreckelsen, it's a hollow cube of white marble and glass measuring 112m on each side – large enough to contain Notre Dame. One of Mitterrand's *grands travaux*, it was opened on 14 July 1989, and forms the current western terminus of the 8km-long **Grand Axe** (Great Axis), which stretches from the Louvre's glass pyramid through the Jardin des Tuileries and along av des Champs Élysées to the Arc de Triomphe, Porte Maillot and finally the foun-

INFORMATION

☎ 01 49 07 27 57
(La Grande Arche)

e www.grandearche.com

Ⓜ La Defénse Grande Arche

🚍 73

🕐 Grande Arche 10am-7pm (last ascent 6pm)

Ⓢ Grande Arche €7/6

ⓘ Info Défense
☎ 01 47 74 84 24, 15 Place de la Défense, 10am-6pm; guides available

Martin Moos

Edward Snyders

Future set in stone.

tains, squares and plazas of La Défense's **Esplanade du Général de Gaulle**. The structure, symbolising a window open to the world, is slightly out of alignment with the Grand Axe.

In a brave attempt to humanise the district's overwhelming corporate feel, the Esplanade and **Parvis** pedestrian precincts are now a **garden of contemporary art** featuring 70 monumental sculptures and murals, including colourful and imaginative works by Calder, Miró and Agam.

DON'T MISS
• CNIT, and Fiat, Manhattan and Elf office buildings • Dôme IMAX cinema • Musée de l'Automobile

HÔTEL DES INVALIDES (3, F5)

The Hôtel des Invalides was built by Louis XIV in the 1670s as a kind of self-contained residential village for up to 4000 *invalides* (disabled veterans); a hundred or so vets are still housed here. The **Cour d'Honneur** courtyard serves as a venue for military parades, overlooked by a statue of Napoleon, affectionately known as the **Little Corporal**.

In the centre of the compound is the glorious **Église du Dôme** (Dome Church; at left), named for its gilded dome which is a glittering landmark. The church, considered one of the finest religious buildings built under Louis XIV, was built between 1677 and 1735; the dome itself took 27 years to build. It was intended for the king's own use and as a royal mausoleum, but instead the church became a mausoleum for military leaders.

In 1861 the Dome Church became home to **Napoleon's tomb**, Napoleon having died on St Helena 40 years earlier. It's an impressive final resting place: Napoleon's body is encased in no fewer than five coffins and a sarcophagus of red porphyry, displayed in an open crypt right under the dome. Other famous personages buried in the church include Napoleon's brother Joseph, military engineer Vauban and WWI hero Marshal Foch.

The buildings on either side of the Cour d'Honneur house the **Musée de l'Armée**, a huge museum of military history from the Stone Age to the end of WWII.

To Arms, Citizens

Unfortunately for Louis XIV's descendants, the Hôtel des Invalides played a key role in the events of 14 July 1789: the Paris mob forced their way into the building and, after fierce fighting, seized 28,000 rifles before heading on to the Bastille prison on the other side of the city. The rest, as they say...

Back from exile: Napoleon's final resting place

LES ÎLES (5, D5)

For most of Paris' 2000-year history the Seine was a major trade route (the city's coat-of-arms still features the medieval boat motif of the Waterman's Guild), and the rivers' two islands – the larger Île de la Cité and the neighbouring Île St-Louis – were the geographical, commercial, religious and political heart of the city. Today the islands, their monuments, bridges and quays are still Paris' most romantic attractions.

Simon Bracken

INFORMATION

✉ 1er, 4e
Ⓜ Cité
✕ see p. 75

The **Île de la Cité** (5, C5), the larger of the Seine's two linked islands, is the historic and tourist centre of Paris. **Notre Dame** (p. 28) is its prime attraction, but gorgeous **Sainte Chapelle** (p. 32), the **Conciergerie**, the **flower market** and the moving **Mémorial des Martyrs de la Déportation** are all worth exploring. Despite its name, the **Pont Neuf** or New Bridge (5, A5) is the oldest of the Seine's 37 bridges (built 1578-1604), and was once lined with houses and shops.

The pretty **Square du Vert Galant**, at the western tip of the island, is the perfect spot for a summer picnic.

Île St-Louis (5, D6), by contrast, has a village-like, provincial calm – ideal for strolling. The island's charming 17th-century stone houses, teahouses, boutiques and upmarket galleries provide a more reflective view of the city. The area around **Pont St-Louis** (linking the two islands) and **Pont Louis-Philippe** is quintessential picture-postcard Paris. The city's best ice cream is sold at **Berthillon**, 31 rue St-Louis en l'Île.

Don't forget to visit the islands after nightfall, when the river shimmers with the watery reflections of their floodlit monuments and bridges.

Island life: the perfect summer refuge

Rob Flynn

DON'T MISS
• secluded place Dauphine • Église St Louis-en-l'Île • Sunday bird market • quayside bouquinistes (bookstalls)

JARDIN DU LUXEMBOURG　　　(5, C2)

When the weather is sunny – or even just not so overcast – Parisians of all ages flock to the formal Franco-Italian-style terraces and chestnut groves of the 25-hectare Jardin du Luxembourg (Luxembourg Gardens) to read, write, relax and sunbathe.

Napoleon dedicated the gardens to the children of Paris, and the gardens still offer all the delights of a Parisian childhood of a century ago. Join *les gosses* (the kids) and rent a model sailing boat at the **Grand Bassin** (the octagonal pond), or cheer the *guignol* (marionettes) at the pint-sized **Théâtre du Luxembourg** – even if you don't understand French.

Next door, there's the modern **playground**, vintage swings and an old-time *carrousel* (merry-go-round). And 100m north of the theatre, kids of up to 35kg can ride Shetland ponies.

In the northwest corner of the gardens, chess and card games – often a dozen at a time – are held every afternoon of the year, rain or shine; BYOB (bring your own board). On the north side of the theatre there are basketball and volleyball courts, or try inviting yourself to a game of *boules* (traditional bowling). There's a popular jogging track around the perimeter.

Less active visitors can simply enjoy the wonderful floral displays (best in spring) or bone-up on their bee-keeping skills at the **apiary**. The ancient *verger* (orchard) contains around 200 varieties of pear and apple trees.

The **Palais du Luxembourg** is at the park's northern edge, with the Italianate Fontaine des Médicis (1642) nearby. The **Musée du Luxembourg** hosts temporary art exhibits, often from different regions of France.

INFORMATION

- ✉ blvd St-Michel, rue de Vaugirard, rue Guynemer, 6e
- ☎ 01 42 34 20 00
- Ⓜ Odéon
- ▣ RER Luxembourg
- ◷ Apr-Oct 7.30am-9.30pm; Nov-Mar 8am-5pm; marionettes Wed, Sat & Sun 3-4pm
- Ⓢ gardens free; playgrounds €2.20; swings or merry-go-round €1.15; pony rides €2.30; boats €2.75/hr; marionettes €3.70
- ⓘ theatre ☎ 01 43 26 46 47; palais ☎ 01 444 61 21 69

Neil Setchfield

Bird in the Hand

As a struggling (and usually famished) young writer, Ernest Hemingway would visit the gardens for dinner – not to build up an appetite by looking at the flowers, but to catch pigeons and take them home to eat.

MUSÉE D'ORSAY   (3, E8)

While the Musée d'Orsay plays second fiddle to the irresistible Louvre, most visitors find it a much more rewarding visit – mostly for its superb collection of French Impressionist and post-Impressionist works.

The museum displays France's national collection of paintings, sculptures, *objets d'art* and other works produced between 1848 and 1914, fitting neatly between that of the Louvre and that of the Centre Pompidou.

The key works are on the ground floor (1848-70) and the upper level (1870-1914). But don't bypass the Rodin sculptures (*Balzac* and *Gates of Hell*) and Art Nouveau collection on the middle level.

The ground floor has an eclectic sculpture gallery; Rude's *Spirit of the Fatherland* is a fragment of his famous *Marseillaise* relief for the Arc de Triomphe, while Carpeaux's exuberant *The Dance* scandalised Paris in 1868. Smaller galleries to each side feature key works from the classical and realist movements, including Ingre's *La Source* and Millet's *The Gleaners*, and some early Impressionist-style works such as Manet's provocative *Olympia* and *Déjeuner sur l'herbe*.

The upper level contains the museum's jewels: dozens of vibrant Impressionist and post-Impressionist works, including Renoir's *Dancing at the Moulin de la Galette*, Degas' *Dance Class*, Monet's *Cathedral of Rouen* series and views of Giverny, van Gogh's self-portraits and *Room at Arles*, and Cézanne's *Card Players*, plus major works by Pisarro, Manet, Whistler (yes, his *Mother*), Gauguin, Sisley and others.

The open-air **terrace** has a great aspect over the Seine and a close-up view of the former station's enormous **clock**.

INFORMATION

- ✉ 1 rue de la Légion d'Honneur, 7e
- ☎ 01 40 49 48 14, 01 45 49 11 11 (recording)
- e www.musee-orsay.fr
- Ⓜ Solférino
- 🚈 RER Musée d'Orsay
- 🚌 24, 63, 68, 69, 73, 83, 84, 94
- ⏰ Tues-Sat 10am-6pm (Thurs to 9.45pm); Sun & June-Sept 9am-6pm
- Ⓢ €6.10/4.60
- ⓘ tours in English Tues-Sat 11am, Thurs 7pm €6.10; 1½hr recorded tours €4.60
- ♿ OK
- ✕ Café des Hauteurs

Sculpture gallery's sensational statuary

Moving Pictures

The Musée d'Orsay's impressive clock gives a clue to its former life – it was a train station, opened at the time of the 1900 universal exposition in Paris. It has also been a hotel and was the film set for Orson Welles' film of Franz Kafka's *The Trial*.

MUSÉE DU LOUVRE (3, E9)

The Louvre may be the world's greatest art museum – but it's probably also the one most avoided by visitors to Paris. Daunted by its sheer size (nearly 750m along the Seine) and overwhelming richness, many people find an afternoon at a smaller gallery far more inviting. But if you have even the merest interest in the fruits of human civilisation from antiquity to the 19th century, then visit you must.

To make your visit more enjoyable, pick up one of the useful map-guides and check out the works you *really* want to see, concentrating on only a couple of sections of the museum.

The most famous works from antiquity include the *Seated Scribe*, the *Jewels of Rameses II* and the armless duo – the *Winged Victory of Samothrace* and the *Venus de Milo*. From the Renaissance, don't miss Michelangelo's *Slaves*, Leonardo da Vinci's *Mona Lisa* and works by Raphael, Botticelli and Titian. French masterpieces of the 19th century include Ingres' *La Grande Odalisque*, Géricault's *The Raft of the Medusa* and the work of David and Delacroix.

The former fortress began its career as a public museum in 1793 with 2500 paintings; now some 30,000 are on display. The 7 billion FF (€1.07 billion) Grand Louvre project has breathed new life into the museum with many new and renovated galleries now open to the public.

To avoid queues at the pyramid entrance, buy your ticket in advance and/or enter through the underground shopping mall.

Simon Bracken

INFORMATION

- ✉ rue de Rivoli, 1er
- ☎ 01 40 20 53 17, 01 40 20 51 51 (recording)
- e www.louvre.fr
- Ⓜ Palais-Royal Musée du Louvre
- 🚌 21, 27, 39, 48, 68, 69, 72, 81, 95
- ⏱ Mon & Wed 9am-9.45pm (some galleries close Mon evening); Thurs-Sun 9am-7pm
- ⑤ €7.50/5 (€5 after 3pm & Sun); free under 18 & 1st Sun of month
- ⓘ tours in English (1½hrs) 3-5/day (Sun 11.30am) €5.80/3.35; audioguides €4.60
- ♿ OK; sculpture gallery for sight-impaired
- ✗ food court, restaurants, cafes

Leda and the Swan, *Musée du Louvre*

Greg Elms

MUSÉE NATIONAL DU MOYEN ÂGE-THERMES DE CLUNY (5, D3)

Here you get two great cultural experiences for the price of one, right in the heart of the city. The National Museum of the Middle Ages is housed in both the remains of the Gallo-Roman baths (built here when Paris was a Roman outpost) and in the late 15th century Hôtel de Cluny, once the home of the Abbots of Cluny – and the finest example of medieval civil architecture in the city.

In an intriguing and intimate space you'll find one of the world's best collections of medieval statuary, illuminated manuscripts, arms, furnishings, and objects made from gold, ivory and enamel. A new display depicts aspects of everyday living during the Middle Ages.

Giraudon / Bridgeman Art Library

INFORMATION

- ✉ 6 Place Paul Painlevé, 5e
- ☎ 01 53 73 78 00
- e www.musee-moyen age.fr
- Ⓜ Cluny-La Sorbonne, St-Michel
- 🚌 21, 27, 38, 63, 85, 86, 87
- ⊘ Wed-Mon 9.15am-5.45pm
- ⓢ €5.50/4 (€4 on Sun; free under 18 & 1st Sun of month)

Bridgeman Giraudon / Lauros / Bridgeman Art Library

Top: The Lady and the Unicorn
Above: The Coronation of Louis XII in 1498

A sublime series of late 15th-century tapestries known as **La Dame à la Licorne** (the Lady with the Unicorn; at left) is hung in a round room on the 1st floor. The series consists of six exquisite pieces – five relating to the senses, the sixth of ambiguous meaning.

A medieval garden and **Forêt de la Licorne** (Unicorn Forest) has recently been laid out along blvd St-Germain based on the illustrations in the tapestries. Entrance to the gardens is free and there's a playground for kids.

The remains of the *frigidarium* (cooling room) of the baths, with its 15m-high vaulted ceiling, is the setting for a number of interesting mosaics and sculptural fragments.

DON'T MISS • the 21 heads of the King's of Judah • stained glass removed from Sainte Chapelle • Golden Rose of Basel, dating from 1330

MUSÉE PICASSO   (5, D8)

Pablo Picasso was the outstanding genius of 20th-century art, and his capacity to work was superhuman: he painted, drew and made things from his early youth until his death, aged nearly 90. Much of his vast legacy can be found in the wonderful Musée Picasso.

INFORMATION

- ✉ 5 rue de Thorigny, 3e
- ☎ 01 42 71 25 21
- Ⓜ St-Paul; Chemin Vert
- ⏲ Wed-Mon 9.30am-6pm (Thurs to 8pm); closes 5.30pm Nov-Mar
- 💲 €4.60/3.05
- ♿ OK
- ✕ cafe in summer

Neil Setchfield

Simon Bracken

Pondering Picasso

Although Picasso (1881-1973) was Spanish, he spent his artistically formative (and *transform*ative) years and much of his later life in Paris. When he died, his family donated a quarter of his entire collection of drawings, engravings, paintings, ceramic works and sculptures to the French government in lieu of inheritance taxes.

In 1985 the government inaugurated the Musée Picasso to display the collection. Although none of his most celebrated works are here, the museum still offers the most comprehensive overview of Picasso's oeuvre – particularly his playfulness and humour.

The 200 paintings of the collection are arranged chronologically, from Picasso's early Blue and Rose periods to the flowering of Cubism and pieces from his later years. Some 3000 drawings and engravings give an insight into the artistic methods and prodigious output of the man, while more than 100 ceramic works and sculptures (many in the garden) demonstrate his mastery of a wide variety of media.

Tucked away in the Marais, the museum is handsomely curated in the **Hôtel Salé**, a carefully restored mid-17th-century mansion. Many of the fine fixtures and pieces of furniture were designed by Diego Giacometti.

The museum also includes the **Picasso Donation** – part of Picasso's personal collection, featuring works by Cézanne, Braque, Matisse and Degas.

DON'T MISS
- Blue Period Self-Portrait • Demoiselles d'Avignon drawings • Still Life with Cane Chair • Young Girl Skipping Rope • Baboon Sculpture with Citroën nose

MUSÉE RODIN (3, F6)

One of the most tranquil spots in the city, the Musée Rodin is also many visitors' favourite Paris museum. When he died, the renowned sculptor Auguste Rodin (1840-1907) left his magnificent 18th-century residence and a huge body of work to the state in lieu of rent. Rooms on two floors of the house display extraordinarily vital bronze and marble sculptures, including casts of some of Rodin's most celebrated works: *The Hand of God*, *St John the Baptist*, *Balzac*, *Cathedral* and *The Kiss* (at right).

Also on display are works by Rodin's model and lover, Camille Claudel (1864-1943), whose more gentle talent was overwhelmed by Rodin's prodigious genius (and his matching temperament). She spent the last 30 years of her life in madness in an asylum on Île St-Louis, unable to work. *L'Age Mûr* (Maturity) is a reflection of her torturous relationship with Rodin; the old woman is his wife.

The museum is housed in the **Hôtel Biron**, a private residence built for a wealthy wig-maker in 1728, and bearing the name of a general who lived here before being guillotined in 1793.

The delightful English-style **rose garden** (the third-largest private garden in Paris) is filled with shade trees and sculptures, including the original version of the work everyone comes to see, *The Thinker*.

Neil Setchfield / Martin Moos

INFORMATION

- ✉ 77 rue de Varenne, 7e
- ☎ 01 44 18 61 10
- e www.musee-rodin.fr
- Ⓜ Varenne
- 🚌 69, 82, 87, 92
- ⏲ 9.30am-5.45pm (winter to 4.45pm), closed Monday; garden closes 6.45pm (5pm winter)
- $ €5/3; gardens only €1
- ♿ limited
- ✗ Caféteria du Musée Rodin

Palatial Hôtel Biron

Thoughtless Step

Rodin's most famous work, *Le Penseur* (The Thinker), was originally intended to grace the steps of the Panthéon – the mausoleum of France's greatest thinkers. But it was rejected by the City of Paris after a full-scale model was pilloried by the public and the press, and attacked by a madman with a hatchet.

Other celebrated works in the garden are *The Burghers of Calais* and the unfinished *Gates of Hell*, which kept Rodin occupied for the last 37 years of his life.

NOTRE DAME (5, C5)

If Paris has a heart, then this is it. Notre Dame de Paris (Our Lady of Paris) is not only a masterpiece of French Gothic architecture, but has also been Catholic Paris' ceremonial focus for seven centuries.

INFORMATION

- ✉ Place du Parvis, 4e
- ☎ 01 42 34 56 10
- Ⓜ Cité
- 🚌 21, 24, 27, 38, 47, 85, 96
- ⏰ cathedral 8am-7pm (closed Sat 12.30-2pm); towers 9.30am-7.30pm (Oct-Mar 10am-5pm); crypt 10am-6pm (Oct-Mar to 5pm); Sun Mass 10 & 11.30am, 12.30pm
- 💲 cathedral free; tower & crypt €5.35/3.80 each
- ⓘ free English-language tours Wed-Thurs noon, Sat 2.30pm (daily Aug)
- ♿ OK for cathedral

Rob Flynn

Simon Bracken

Ghoulish guardians

Built between 1163 and 1345 on a site occupied first by a Roman temple then by two earlier Christian churches, the cathedral was badly damaged following the Revolution; extensive renovations were made in the 19th century, partly due to the goading of Victor Hugo in his novel *The Hunchback of Notre Dame*.

The building is remarkable for its sublime balance, although if you look closely you'll notice minor asymmetrical elements introduced to avoid monotony. The cathedral's immense interior, a marvel of medieval engineering, can accommodate over 6000 worshippers. Exceptional features include the 7800-pipe **organ** and the spectacular **rose windows**, the most renowned of which are the window over the west facade (a full 10m across) and that on the north side of the transept, which has remained virtually unchanged since the 13th century.

Climbing the 387 steps of the **north tower** (entrance on rue du Cloître Notre Dame) brings you to the top of the **west facade**, where you'll find yourself face to face with many of the cathedral's most frightening gargoyles, which enjoy a spectacular view of Paris.

The best view of the **flying buttresses** – a Gothic technical innovation used to support the sheer walls and roof of the chancel – is from **Square Jean XXIII**, the lovely little park behind the cathedral.

Where Time Stands Still

Distances from Paris to every part of France are measured from place du Parvis Notre Dame. A bronze star, set in the pavement adjacent to the cathedral's main entrance, marks the exact location of *point zero des routes de France*.

PARC DE LA VILLETTE (2, A13)

This futuristic park in the city's forgotten far-northeastern corner is a playground for kids and adults alike. The park opened in 1993, and its lawns are enlivened by walkways, imaginative public furniture, a series of themed gardens and whimsical bright-red building-sculptures, known as *folies*. Attractions for the kids include a **merry-go-round**, a **playground** and two large play areas.

The centrepiece of the park, however, is the enormous **Cité des Sciences et de l'Industrie**, an interactive science museum, complete with planetarium, aquarium, cinema and multimedia library.

The adjacent **Géode** is a spectacular 36m-diameter sphere, whose mirror-like surface (made up of thousands of highly polished, stainless-steel triangles) has made it one of the architectural calling cards of modern Paris. Inside is an Omnimax cinema, where high-resolution films projected onto a semispherical, 180° screen give viewers a real sense of being part of the action.

The **Cinaxe**, nearby, is a 60-seat hydraulic cinema that moves in synchronisation with the action on the screen (space flight, Formula 1 racing etc).

INFORMATION

- ✉ 30 av Corentin-Cariou, 19e
- ☎ 01 40 05 80 00 CSI & Géode; 01 44 84 44 84 Cité de la Musique
- e www.la-villette.com; www.cite-sciences.fr; www.cite-musique.fr
- Ⓜ Porte de la Villette; Porte de Pantin
- 🚌 75, 150, 152, 250A
- ⏱ CSI Tues-Sun 10am-6pm (Sun to 7pm); Géode Tues-Sun 10.30am-9.30pm (Sun to 7.30pm), 45min films every hr; Cinaxe 11am-5pm, 5min films every 15mins
- ⑤ Cité Pass €8/6; Cité des Enfants €5.05 adult + 2 children; Cinaxe €5.20/4.45
- ⓘ Information folie ☎ 01 40 03 75 03
- ♿ OK
- ✗ cafes & fast-food folie

Martin Moos

The **Cité de la Musique**, towards the south of the park, houses a **music museum** with over 4500 instruments from the 16th century until today, a **concert hall** and the National Conservatory of Dance and Music.

Olivier Cirendini

Parc de la Villette's futuristic architecture

DON'T MISS
- open-air cinema • Jardin des Frayeurs Enfantines (Garden of Childhood Frights) • Cité des Enfants • Maison de la Villette – history of the site • Bicyclette Ensevelie (Buried Bicycle) sculpture

PLACE DES VOSGES & THE MARAIS (5, C8)

The Place des Vosges and the surrounding Marais quarter is arguably Paris' most charming and compelling neighbourhood. Its pre-Revolutionary architecture and narrow streets perfectly complement the dozens of bars, boutiques and restaurants that have blossomed here in recent years.

In the early 1600s, Henri IV built the Place Royal, creating Paris' most fashionable residential district. This elegant square (now known as the **Place des Vosges**) is a quadrangle of 36 symmetrical houses with ground-floor arcades, steep slate roofs and large dormer windows. The lovely park in the centre was once used for jousting and fighting duels, but today the park and

Rob Flynn

the surrounding arcades are used for more refined pursuits. For a peek inside, visit the **Maison de Victor Hugo** (6 Place des Vosges), where Victor Hugo lived from 1832 to 1848 (now a museum).

The surrounding marsh (*marais*) was drained, and wealthy aristocrats soon built their luxurious but subtle *hôtels particuliers* (private mansions) nearby; many of these now house museums and government institutions – the **Musée Picasso** (p. 26), the **Musée Carnavalet** (p. 36) and the **Archives Nationales** are fine examples.

The Marais also has a long-established **Jewish quarter** around the rue des Rosiers and rue des Écouffes. The **synagogue** in rue Pavée was designed by Hector Guimard.

Partly as a result of the deportation of the Jewish residents during the Nazi occupation, the Marais became one of the most neglected neighbourhoods of Paris. But today it bustles with life and is the centre of Paris' vibrant gay community. For a walk around Marais, see page 49.

Simon Bracken

Sit and regain your balance in Place des Vosges' symmetrical surrounds.

DON'T MISS
• Hôtel de Sully • a nightcap at Le Petit Fer à Cheval
• boutiques along rue Vieille du Temple & rue des Francs Bourgeois

SACRÉ CŒUR & MONTMARTRE (4, C6)

Perched on the summit of the Butte de Montmartre, the immense wedding-cake **Basilique du Sacré Cœur** (Basilica of the Sacred Heart) is one of Paris' most recognisable landmarks – visible from vantage points throughout the city. Although it may appear much older, the basilica was consecrated in 1919 as an act of contrition following the humiliating Franco-Prussian war of 1870-1.

Some 234 spiralling steps lead you to the basilica's **dome**, which affords one of Paris' most spectacular panoramas – up to 30km on a clear day.

The basilica itself is worth a cursory glance inside, but the steps leading down the hill in front of it are where the action takes place – lovers, buskers, locals and foreigners come here to take in the vistas and photograph each other. If you want to pray, ancient **St-Pierre de Montmartre**, adjacent to the basilica, is a much more tranquil spot.

Despite the throngs, the **Butte de Montmartre** (Montmartre Hill, the highest point in Paris) retains much of its bohemian village feel. In its twisting, narrow streets you'll find Paris' two surviving **windmills** (4, B4), and sole **vineyard** (4, B5; on rue des Saules). Lose yourself in the area's **cobblestone streets**, far from the Paris of traffic and crowds.

INFORMATION

Ⓜ Abbesses; Blanche; Pigalle
🚌 30, 54, 67, 80, 95

Rob Flynn

Liberty before the Sacred Heart

As you elbow your way through the gaggle of bus-delivered tourists paying outrageous prices for corny, mass-produced paintings in the nearby **Place du Tertre**, it's difficult to imagine Van Gogh, Renoir, Picasso and Dalí setting up their easels here to change the face of modern art.

For a walk around Montmartre, see page 51.

Headless on Montmartre

Saint Denis, patron saint of France, introduced Christianity to Paris in the 2nd century. He was beheaded by the Romans on the hill now named Montmartre (Martyr Hill). You'll often see statues of him holding his head under his arm (for example on Notre Dame's portal).

SAINTE CHAPELLE   (5, B5)

The most exquisite of Paris' Gothic monuments is tucked away within the walls of the **Palais de Justice** (Law Courts).

In contrast to the buttressed bulk of nearby Notre Dame, Sainte Chapelle is a masterpiece of delicacy and finesse. The 'walls' of the **upper chapel** (built for worship by the king and his court) are sheer curtains of richly coloured and finely detailed **stained glass**, which bathe the chapel in an extraordinary light. Designed to inspire religious awe, the effect is still mesmerising.

INFORMATION

- ✉ Palais de Justice, blvd du Palais, 1er
- ☎ 01 53 73 78 50
- Ⓜ Cité
- 🚌 21, 27, 38, 85, 96
- ⏲ Apr-Sept 9.30am-6.30pm; Oct-Mar 10am-4.30pm
- Ⓢ €5.35/3.50
- ♿ limited

Martin Moos

The windows depict biblical scenes, from Genesis (on the left as you enter the chapel) to the Apocalypse (the **rose window** behind you). The windows directly behind the altar depict Christ's Passion. Some 720 of the 1134 scenes depicted in the windows are the original stained glass – the oldest in Paris.

Built in just three years (compared with nearly 200 for Notre Dame), Sainte Chapelle was consecrated in 1248. The chapel was conceived by Louis IX (St Louis) to house his collection of holy relics, including the alleged Crown of Thorns and part of John the Baptist's skull (for which he paid several times the cost of building the chapel itself). The relics were displayed on the wooden **canopied platform** in front of the altar, but the reliquary was destroyed during the Revolution and the relics relocated to Notre Dame.

On the right-hand side of the chapel, near the altar, is the **oratory**, where Louis would privately attend Mass without having to face his less-than-devout courtiers.

Martin Moos

Inspirational old glass

DON'T MISS
- evening medieval concerts • statues of the apostles • 75m spire
- window depicting the life of Moses

TOUR EIFFEL (3, F2)

It may have become the ubiquitous icon of mass tourism, but even the most jaded visitor is guaranteed to feel a *frisson* of excitement walking down the **Champ de Mars** towards the Tour Eiffel (Eiffel Tower).

By day, the tower is awesome: its massive size, its shape and its elemental construction make it as obvious a symbol of national potency today as when it was built to commemorate the centenary of the Revolution for the 1889 Exposition Universelle (World Fair).

At night, transformed by clever illumination, it floats on the edge of the Seine as if built of nothing more substantial than filaments of light.

Named for its designer, Gustave Eiffel, the tower reaches a height of 320m, including the television antenna at the very tip. This figure can vary by as much as 15cm, as the 7000-tonne tower of iron – held together by 2.5 million rivets – expands in warm weather and contracts when it's cold. It was the world's tallest structure until Manhattan's Chrysler Building was completed in 1930.

When you're done peering upwards through the girders, take in the **panoramic views** from any of the three levels (at 57m, 115m and a heart-stopping 276m) open to the public. On a clear day (infrequent in Paris) the view from the top extends some 60km. If you're fit, you can avoid the lift queues by walking up the stairs in the south pillar to the 1st or 2nd platforms.

INFORMATION

✉ Champ de Mars, 7e
☎ 01 44 11 23 23
🄴 www.tour-eiffel.fr
Ⓜ Bir Hakeim; Trocadéro
🚆 RER Champ de Mars
🚌 42, 69, 72, 82, 87
🕐 9.30am-11pm (mid-June-Aug 9am-midnight)
⑤ lift to 1st flr €3.70/2.15; 2nd flr €6.90/3.80; 3rd flr €9.90/5.35; stairway to 1st/2nd flrs €3.05
♿ limited to 1st & 2nd flrs
🍴 1st flr cafe & Altitude 95 bar/restaurant; 2nd flr Jules Verne restaurant

Richard I'Anson

The view up the Tour Eiffel

DON'T MISS
• views at dusk • post office on the 2nd level
• Gustave Eiffel's 3rd flr office • picnic in the Champs de Mars

sights & activities

Some of the oldest and most interesting of Paris' quartiers – as well as many of its major monuments and sights – are strung along the banks of the Seine, between Pont de Sully in the east and Pont de la Concorde in the west. And the romantic beauty and monuments of the Seine's two islands, Île de la Cité and Île St-Louis (3, G12; p.21), makes them a natural magnet for visitors.

Today the Right Bank is where it's all happening. In the last decade the former working-class areas of the **Bastille** (3, G15) and **Marais** (5, C8) – and **Belleville** (2, D12) and **Ménilmontant** (2, E13) further north-east – have become the epicentre of a renewed urban spirit in Paris, with their avant-garde galleries, theatres and boutiques, and legions of bars, cafes and eateries.

If it's traditional big-city bustle you're craving, head for the department stores and international brand names on **rue de Rivoli** (5, B6) the department stores of the **Grands Boulevards** near Opéra (3, B9) or the pedestrianised shopping area around **Les Halles** (5, A7) and the intriguing **Montorgueil** quarter (3, D11).

The chic end of town is a little further west – around **Place Vendôme** (3, C8), **Opéra** (3, B9) and the **Champs Elysées** (3, C5) – where you can visit some of the most gorgeous boutiques on earth.

On the Left Bank you'll find all manner of bookshops, cinemas and cafes in the narrow streets of the **Quartier Latin** (5, D3). In recent years the area around **St-Germain** and **St-Sulpice** (3, G9) has become a chic shopping neighbourhood (and it's the American epicentre of Paris), and close by there's **Odéon** (3, G10), with its cinemas, cafes, clubs, crowds and collectibles.

Off the Beaten Track

Hidden near the western end of the Île de la Cité is **Place Dauphine** (5, A5; Ⓜ Pont Neuf), Paris' oldest square, a surprisingly restful spot in the heart of the city. And just metres from the throbbing traffic at Bastille is peaceful **Port de l'Arsenal** (3, H15) – a pleasant place to stroll or picnic with the kids.

Further afield, **La Butte aux Cailles** or Quail Hill (2, J10; Ⓜ Place d'Italie or Corvisart) retains a 19th-century village feel with picturesque cobbled streets, old houses and bohemian cafes and restaurants. Or picnic in lovely **Parc Montsouris** (2, K9; Ⓜ Cité Universitaire) and explore the old-fashioned cottages and artists' studios around cobbled Square de Montsouris.

Canal St-Martin: compact and populous Paris has many tranquil bolt holes.

Rob Flynn

MUSEUMS

For other museum listings, see the key museums (pp.23-7 & 29) and Paris for Children and Quirky Paris later this chapter (pp. 44-5).

Musée de l'Armée

(3, F5) Everything you wanted to know about warfare but were afraid to ask, from Stone Age stick-throwing to WWI mustard gas. There's perhaps a few too many weapons, flags and medals, but Vizier, Napoleon's stuffed horse, is a crowd-pleaser.

✉ **Hôtel National des Invalides, 129 rue de Grenelle, 7e**
☎ **01 44 42 37 72**
🌐 **www.invalides.org**
Ⓜ **La Tour Maubourg**
🚌 **24, 49, 63, 80, 87, 93**
🕐 **summer 10am-6pm, winter 10am-5pm**
💲 **€6.10/4.57** ♿

Musée d'Art et d'Histoire (1, B7)

This Saint Denis museum, located 10km north of the centre, occupies a restored Carmelite convent founded in 1625. It includes reconstructions of the Carmelites' cells, an 18th-century apothecary, and artefacts found during excavations around the area. Consider this as a definite side-trip if you go up to Saint Denis to visit the Basilique (p. 40).

✉ **22bis rue Gabriel Péri, St-Denis** ☎ **01 42 43 05 10** Ⓜ **St-Denis-Basilique (line 13)**
🚌 **255, 256** 🕐 **Mon, Wed, Fri 10am-5.30pm, Thurs 10am-8pm, Sat-Sun 2-6.30pm**
💲 **€3.05/1.55** ♿ limited

Musée d'Art et d'Histoire du Judaisme (5, B8)

Situated in a 17th-century mansion in the heart of the Marais, this museum recounts the history and everyday reality of Judaism, especially in France. Includes documents on the Dreyfus Affair as well as works by Chagall and Modigliani.

✉ **Hôtel de St-Aignan, 71 rue du Temple, 3e**
☎ **01 53 01 86 53**
🌐 **www.mahj.org**
Ⓜ **Arts et Métiers**
🚌 **38, 39, 47** 🕐 **Mon-Fri 11am-6pm, Sun 10am-6pm** 💲 **€6.10/3.80** ♿

Musée des Arts d'Afrique et d'Océanie (2, H15)

This unusual museum has something for everyone – incredibly expressive African tribal art, Australian Aboriginal art, colonial architecture, Art Deco furnishings – and an aquarium full of tropical fish and crocodiles in the basement!

✉ **293 av Daumesnil, 12e** ☎ **01 43 46 51 61**
Ⓜ **Porte Dorée** 🚌 **46**
🕐 **Wed-Mon 10am-5.30pm** 💲 **€4.60/3.05** ♿ limited

Musée des Arts Décoratifs (3, D9)

Rich, diverse collection of furniture, furnishings, jewellery and *objets d'art* (such as ceramics and glassware) from the Middle Ages and the Renaissance through to the Art Nouveau and Art Deco periods.

✉ **Palais du Louvre, 107 rue de Rivoli, 1er**
☎ **01 44 55 57 50**
🌐 **www.ucad.fr**
Ⓜ **Palais Royal** 🚌 **21, 27, 39, 48, 68, 69, 72, 81** 🕐 **Tues-Sun 11am-6pm (Wed to 9pm)**
💲 **€5.35/3.80 (incl Musée de la Mode et du Textile; p. 36)** ♿

Musée des Arts et Métiers (5, A9)

A compelling history of machines and instruments (18-20th century) for anyone with a scientific bent. In pride of place is Foucault's original pendulum, which he introduced to the world with the words, 'Come and

Old money: the franc and other extinct currencies.

see the world turn'.
✉ **60 rue Réaumur, 3e**
☎ **01 53 01 82 20**
ℯ **www.cnam.fr/mus
eum ⓜ Arts et Métiers**
🚌 **21, 27, 38, 39, 47**
🕐 **Tues-Sun 10am-6pm
(Thurs to 9.30pm)**
⑨ **€5.35/3.80** ♿

Musée Carnavalet-Musée de l'Histoire de Paris (5, D8)
Worth visiting just for the two charming *hôtels partic-uliers* in which it's housed, this compelling museum illuminates the history of Paris from the Gallo-Roman period to the 20th century. Noteworthy exhibits include the keys to the Bastille, Napoleon's cradle and Proust's cork-lined bedroom.
✉ **23 rue de Sévigné,
3e** ☎ **01 44 59 58 58**
ℯ **www.paris-france
.org/musees ⓜ St-Paul,
Chemin Vert**
🚌 **29, 69, 76, 96**
🕐 **Tues-Sun 10am-5pm**
⑨ **€5.35/3.80** ♿ **limited**

Musée de la Curiosité et de la Magie (5, E7)
A delightful museum for kids of all ages interested in the ancient arts of magic, optical illusions and sleight of hand. Located in the *caves* of the house of the Marquis de Sade.
✉ **11 rue St-Paul, 4e**
☎ **01 42 72 13 26**
ⓜ **St-Paul**

🚌 **67, 69, 76, 96**
🕐 **Wed & Sat-Sun 2-7pm** ⑨ **€6.90/4.60
(includes magic show)**

Musée Edith Piaf
(2, E12) Die-hard fans of *la môme piaf* (the urchin sparrow) won't regret a thing about a visit to this tiny little museum in the working-class district of Belleville where she was born and began her career. Packed with memorabilia and lovingly tended; visits by prior appointment only.
✉ **5 rue Crespin du Gast,
11e** ☎ **01 43 55 52 72**
ⓜ **Ménilmontant** 🚌 **96**
🕐 **Mon-Thurs 1-6pm**
⑨ **donation**

Musée Guimet/Musée des Arts Asiatiques (3, D2)
Europe's most outstanding museum of Asian treasures includes sublime pieces from former French Indochina. If the museum has whetted your appetite for Asian art, don't miss Emile Guimet's original collection of Chinese and Japanese Buddhas in the nearby Musée du Panthéon Bouddhique.
✉ **6 Place d'Iéna, 19
av d'Iéna, 16e**
☎ **01 56 52 53 00**
ℯ **www.museeguimet
.fr ⓜ Iéna** 🚌 **22, 30,
32, 63, 82** 🕐 **Wed-Sun
10am-6pm** ⑨ **€5.50/4**

Musée de l'Homme
(3, E1) If you've never been to Easter Island, you can find one of those colossal heads in the Museum of Mankind. Fascinating exhibits cover human evolution, anthropology and culture over the past 3½ million years or so. Housed in the Palais de Chaillot, the museum has exhibits from Africa, Asia, Europe, the Arctic, the Pacific and the Americas.
✉ **Palais de Chaillot,
17 Place du Trocadéro,
16e** ☎ **01 44 05 72 72**
ℯ **www.mnhn.fr**
ⓜ **Trocadéro**
🚌 **22, 30, 32, 63, 72, 82**
🕐 **Wed-Mon 9am-5pm**
⑨ **€4.60/3.05** ♿

Musée de la Mode et du Textile (3, D9)
This is a fascinating history of what Paris does best – fabrics, clothing and accessories from the 18th century to Dior, Schiaparelli and Paco Rabanne. More than 200,000 fashion images complement the exhibits.
✉ **Palais du Louvre,
107 rue de Rivoli, 1er**
☎ **01 44 55 57 50**
ℯ **www.ucad.fr**
ⓜ **Palais Royal**
🚌 **21, 27, 39, 48, 68,
69, 72, 81, 95**
🕐 **Tues-Fri 11am-6pm**
⑨ **€5.35/3.80
(incl Musée des Arts
Décoratifs; p. 35)** ♿

Musée de la Monnaie
(5, A4) If you like your money old, spend some time in the former national mint (built 1770), which displays coins and medals from antiquity to the present as well as presses and other minting equipment.
✉ **11 Quai de Conti,
6e** ☎ **01 40 46 55 35**

Museums Pass
If you plan to 'do' multiple museums and monuments over just a few days, or want to avoid long queues, invest in a **Carte Musée et Monuments** (€13/25.20/39 for 1/3/5 days), available from major metro stations, participating museums and tourist offices. The pass doesn't cover tours or special exhibitions.

e www.monnaie
deparis.fr ⓜ Pont Neuf
🚌 27, 58, 70 🕐 Tues-
Fri 11am-5.30pm, Sat-
Sun 12-5.30pm; mint
tours Wed & Fri 2.15pm
⑤ €3.80/2.30; free 1st
Sun of month ♿ limited

Musée National des Arts et Traditions Populaires (2, C3)

The National Museum of Popular Arts and Traditions has displays illustrating life in rural France before and during the Industrial Revolution. If you've had a surfeit of kings, emperors and *hôtels particuliers*, the antidote is this view of how the other half – the rural poor – lived, worked and played in pre-industrial France.

✉ 6 av du Mahatma Gandhi, 16e ☎ 01 44 17 60 00 e www.culture .fr/culture/atp/mnatp ⓜ Les Sablons 🚌 73, 244 🕐 Wed-Mon 9.30am-5.15pm ⑤ €3.80/2.60 ♿

Martin Moos

Eugène Delacroix the romantic

Musée National Eugène Delacroix

(3, G9) Delacroix, leader of the romantic school of painting, moved to this apartment/studio while he painted the murals in nearby Église St-Sulpice, and he remained here until his death in 1863. You'll see some minor works, sketches and the artist's personal mementoes.

✉ 6 Place de Furstemberg, 6e ☎ 01 44 41 86 50 e www.musee-dela croix.fr ⓜ Mabillon, St-Germain des Prés 🚌 39, 48, 63, 95 🕐 Wed-Mon 9.30am-5pm ⑤ €3.50/2.30 ♿ limited

Musée de la Serrure-Bricard (5, D8)

The Lock Museum showcases locks, keys and door knockers from ancient to modern times. Security conscious? Check out the lock that traps your hand in the jaws of a bronze lion if you insert the wrong key.

✉ 1 rue de la Perle, 3e ☎ 01 42 77 79 62 ⓜ St-Paul, Chemin Vert 🚌 29 🕐 Mon 2-5pm, Tues-Fri 10am-noon & 2-5pm ⑤ €4.60/2.30 ♿ limited

GALLERIES

Parisians don't make a strong distinction between museums and galleries: works are often housed in buildings at least as interesting as the works themselves. The galleries listed below all have permanent collections; *Pariscope* and *L'Officiel des Spectacles* list temporary and travelling exhibitions.

Espace Montmartre Salvador Dalí (4, C5)

Over 300 works by Salvador Dalí (1904-89), the flamboyant Catalan surrealist printmaker, painter, sculptor and self-promoter, are on display at this museum around the corner from Place du Tertre.

✉ 9-11 rue Poulbot, 14e ☎ 01 42 64 40 10 e www.dali-espace montmartre.com ⓜ Abbesses 🚌 64, 80

🕐 10am-6.30pm (summer until 9pm) ⑤ €6.10/4.60 ♿ limited

Fondation Cartier pour l'Art Contemporain (2, H9)

Brought to you by the designer watch and jewellery people, this conceptual gallery and performance space shows contemporary art, design and installations; the stunningly

modern digs are by designer-architect Jean Nouvel (of Institut du Monde Arabe fame) with designer garden by Lothar Baumgarten.

✉ 261 blvd Raspail, 6e ☎ 01 42 18 56 50 e www.fondation .cartier.fr ⓜ Raspail 🚌 38, 68, 91 🕐 12-8pm; Nomad Soirée (live performance) Thurs 8.30pm ⑤ €5.30/3.80 ♿

Maison Européenne de la Photographie

(5, D7) The Maison Européenne de la Photographie, housed in an 18th-century *hôtel particulier*, has permanent and temporary exhibits, an excellent Polaroid gallery, and a permanent homage to Irving Penn.

✉ 5-7 rue de Fourcy, 4e ☎ 01 44 78 75 00 e www.mep-fr.org Ⓜ St-Paul, Pont Marie 🚌 67, 69, 96, 76 🕐 Wed-Sun 11am-7.45pm ⑤ €5.30/3.05 ♿ magnifier for sight-impaired

Musée d'Art Moderne de la Ville de Paris

(3, D3) If you like skateboarding and big art, the Palais de Tokyo is your kind of gallery. Dufy's *Fée Électricité* is said to be the world's biggest picture; *La Danse* by Matisse isn't far behind. You'll also find Fauvism, Cubism, Surrealism and abstraction in abundance.

✉ 11 av du Président Wilson, 16e ☎ 01 53 67 40 00 e www.paris-france .org/musees Ⓜ Iéna, Alma-Marceau 🚌 42, 63, 72, 80, 92 🕐 10am-5.30pm (to 7pm Sat-Sun) ⑤ €4.60/3.05 (Sun free before 1pm) ♿

Musée d'Art Naïf Max Fourny (4, D7)

The vivid paintings in the Museum of Naive Art, from around the world, have an immediate appeal, thanks in part to their whimsical and generally optimistic perspective on life.

✉ Halle St-Pierre, 2 rue Ronsard, 18e ☎ 01 42 58 72 89

e www.hallestpierre .org Ⓜ Anvers 🚌 30, 54, 84 🕐 10am-6pm (closed Aug) ⑤ €6.10/4.60 ♿ limited

Dali dalliance.

Rob Flynn

Musée Gustave Moreau (2, C9)

Housed in the symbolist artist's former apartment and studio (complete with gorgeous spiral staircase), this quirky museum is crammed with thousands of paintings, drawings and sketches of Moreau's (1826-98) favourite mythological and fantastic subjects.

✉ 14 rue de La Rochefoucauld, 9e ☎ 01 48 74 38 50 Ⓜ Trinité 🚌 26, 32, 43, 68, 81 🕐 Mon & Wed 11am-5pm, Thurs-Sun 10am-12.30pm & 2-5pm ⑤ €3.35/2.30 ♿ limited

Musée Jacquemart-André (3, A5)

This enviable private art collection in an elegant townhouse is noted for its paintings by Rembrandt and van Dyck, and the Italian Renaissance works of Bernini, Botticelli, Carpaccio, Donatello,

Mantegna, Tintoretto, Titian and Uccello. The free audioguide explains the collection in detail.

✉ 158 blvd Haussmann, 8e ☎ 01 42 89 04 91 e www.musee-jacque mart-andre.com Ⓜ St-Philippe du Roule 🚌 22, 28, 43, 52, 54, 80, 83, 84, 93 🕐 10am-6pm ⑤ €7.65/5.80 ♿

Musée Marmottan-Claude Monet (2, E3)

The Marmottan-Claude Monet Museum has not only the world's largest collection of works by the Impressionist Claude Monet – including *Impression Soleil Levant* (which gave the Impressionists their name) and a magnificent water-lily series – but also the exquisite 13th-century Wildenstein illuminated manuscripts, major Impressionist pieces and Gauguin and Renoir paintings.

✉ 2 rue Louis-Boilly, 16e ☎ 01 42 24 07 02 e www.marmottan .com Ⓜ La Muette 🚌 22, 32, 52 🕐 Tues-Sun 10am-5.30pm ⑤ €6.10/3.80 ♿

Musée de l'Orangerie

(3, D7) The collection of 144 so-so Impressionist works is eclipsed by Monet's astonishing *Water Lilies* – eight huge panels conceived for the oval basement rooms of this former Tuileries greenhouse. Closed for renovation at time of writing.

✉ Jardin des Tuileries, 1er ☎ 01 42 97 48 16 Ⓜ Concorde 🚌 24, 42, 52, 72, 73, 84, 94 🕐 Wed-Mon 9.45am-5.15pm ⑤ €4.60/3.05 ♿

NOTABLE BUILDINGS

Bibliothèque Nationale de France – François-Mitterrand

(2, H12) The National Library has more than 10 million books and historical documents shelved in its four strikingly modern 80m-high towers, resembling open books.
✉ 11 Quai François Mauriac, 13e ☎ 01 53 79 49 49 e www.bnf.fr ⓪ Quai de la Gare, Bibliothèque F Mitterrand ⏲ Tues-Sat 9am-7pm, Sun 12-7pm ⑤ free ♿

Conciergerie (5, B5)

The fairy-tale Conciergerie building was a royal palace in the 14th century, before becoming a prison, torture chamber and lockup for nearly 3000 victims of the guillotine. The **Tour de l'Horloge** houses Paris' first public clock (1370).
✉ 1 Quai de l'Horloge, 1er ☎ 01 53 73 78 50 ⓪ Cité 🚌 21, 24, 27, 38, 58, 70, 81 ⏲ summer 9.30am-6.30pm, winter 10am-5pm ⑤ €5.35/3.50; €7.65 with Ste-Chapelle (p. 30) ♿ limited

Hôtel de Sully (5, E7)

The Hôtel de Sully is a superb, early 17th-century aristocratic mansion. The late Renaissance-style courtyards are adorned with bas-reliefs of the seasons and the elements. Temporary photographic exhibitions are held in the *orangerie*.
✉ 62 rue St-Antoine, 4e ☎ 01 44 61 20 00 ⓪ St-Paul 🚌 20, 29, 65, 69, 76 ⏲ garden 9am-7pm; info centre/library Tues-Sat 10am-7pm ⑤ free; fee for exhibitions ♿ limited

Hôtel de Ville (5, C6)

Paris' city hall was rebuilt in the neo-Renaissance style between 1874 and 1882 after having been gutted during the Paris Commune (1871). The ornate facade is decorated with 108 statues of noteworthy Parisians.
✉ Place de l'Hôtel de Ville, 4e ☎ 01 42 76 50 49 e www.parisfrance.org ⓪ Hôtel de Ville 🚌 67, 69, 76 ♿ limited

Institut du Monde Arabe (5, E5)

The striking facade has thousands of aperture-like windows which regulate light and heat. On the 7th floor is a museum of 9th to 19th-century art and artisanship from all over the Arab world, while the teahouse on the 9th floor has great views.
✉ 1 rue des Fossés St-Bernard, 5e ☎ 01 40 51 38 38 e www.imarabe.org ⓪ Cardinal Lemoine, Jussieu 🚌 24, 63, 67, 86, 87, 89 ⏲ Tues-Sun 10am-6pm ⑤ building free; museum €3.80/3.05 ♿

Opéra Bastille (3, G15)

Inaugurated on the 200th anniversary of the storming of the Bastille, Paris' high-tech 'second' opera house has weathered political fallout and technical problems to become a concert favourite. See also p. 90.
✉ 2-6 Place de la Bastille, 11e ☎ 01 40 01 19 70 e www.opera-de-paris .fr ⓪ Bastille 🚌 20, 29, 65, 69, 76, 86, 87, 91 ⏲ guided tours: phone for information ⑤ €9.15/6.90 ♿

Opéra Garnier (3, B9)

Now home to ballet rather than opera (see p. 91), this grandiose theatre was designed by 35-year-old Charles Garnier to trumpet Napoleon III's Second Empire. Chagall redecorated the auditorium ceiling in 1964.
✉ Place de l'Opéra, 9e ☎ 01 40 01 22 63 e www.opera-de-paris .fr ⓪ Opéra

Exquisite window into the Arab world

Simon Bracken

🚌 20, 21, 22, 27, 29, 42, 52, 53, 66 ⏰ 10am-5pm (to 6pm summer) 💲 €9.15/6.90 ♿ limited

Palais de Chaillot

(3, D1) The distinctive curved, colonnaded wings of the *palais*, built for the World Exhibition of 1937, house four museums – including the **Musée de l'Homme** (p. 36). The terrace has an exceptional panorama of the Jardins du Trocadéro, the Seine and the Tour Eiffel.
✉ **Place du Trocadéro, 16e** Ⓜ **Trocadéro** 🚌 **22, 30, 32, 63** ⏰ **10am-5pm** 💲 **€7/5.50** ♿

Panthéon (5, D3)

The Panthéon's dome dominates the Quartier Latin.

Inside are the mortal remains of 62 'great men', including Voltaire, Rousseau, Louis Braille, Victor Hugo, Émile Zola... and Marie Curie.
✉ **Place du Panthéon, 5e** ☎ **01 44 32 18 00** Ⓜ **Cardinal Lemoine** 🚌 **84, 89** ⏰ **summer 9.30am-6.30pm, winter 10am-6.15pm** 💲 **€6.40/4**

Tour Montparnasse

(3, K7) It may be a boring office block – but the panoramic view of Paris from the 56th floor and roof of Paris' tallest building are unbeatable – not least because you also get to see the Tour Eiffel.
✉ **rue de l'Arrivée, 15e** ☎ **01 45 38 52 56** 🇪 **www.tourmont parnasse56.com**

Ⓜ **Montparnasse Bienvenüe** 🚌 **28, 48, 89, 91, 92, 94, 95, 96** ⏰ **summer 9.30am-11pm, winter to 10pm** 💲 **€7.65/6.40/5.20**

Tour de Jean Sans Peur (3, D11)

The 6-floor, 29m Gothic tower of 'John without fear' was built by the Duc de Bourogne in the early 15th century so he could hide at the top, safe from his enemies. It has recently opened to visitors.
✉ **20 rue Étienne Marcel, 2e** ☎ **01 40 26 20 28** Ⓜ **Étienne Marcel** 🚌 **29, 38, 47, 75** ⏰ **Thurs, Sat & Sun (Tues-Sun school holidays) 1.30-6pm** 💲 **€5.35/3.80**

PLACES OF WORSHIP

Cathédrale-Basilique Saint Denis (1, B7)

For 1200 years – from Dagobert I (629-39) to Louis XVIII (1814-24) – this was the burial place of the kings of France, and a place of pilgrimage for living kings and popes. The ornate royal tombs are adorned with some truly remarkable statuary, and the basilica that contains them was world's first major Gothic structure. While you are there, visit the Musée d-Art et d'Historie (p. 35).
✉ **Nécropole des rois de France, rue de Strasbourg 93200, St-Denis** ☎ **01 48 09 83 54, tourist info 01 55 87 08 70** Ⓜ **St-Denis-Basilique (line 13)** 🚌 **255, 256** ⏰ **10am-4.30pm (Sun from noon, Apr-Sept to 6.30pm)** 💲 **nave free; transept**

& chancel €5.50/3.20 ♿ limited

Église St-Étienne du Mont (5, E3)

The carved rood screen is the only one remaining in Paris. Relics of Sainte Geneviève (patron saint of Paris) are in the ambulatory, and a plaque on the floor marks the spot where a defrocked priest killed a bishop in 1857.
✉ **Place Ste-Geneviève, 5e** Ⓜ **Cardinal Lemoine** 🚌 **84, 89** ⏰ **Mon-Sat 8am-7pm, Sun 9am-7pm** 💲 **free** ♿

Église St-Eustache

(3, D11) Louis XIV celebrated his first communion in this beautiful church, a mixture of Gothic design and Renaissance decoration. Liszt and Berlioz both premiered new works here,

and the church is still renowned for its choral and organ music.
✉ **Place du Jour, 1er** Ⓜ **Les Halles** 🚌 **38, 47, 74** ⏰ **Mon-Sat 9am-7pm, Sun 8.15am-12.30pm & 2.30-7pm; Mass with Gregorian chant Sun 11am** 💲 **free** ♿

Église St-Germain des Prés (5, A3)

The oldest church in Paris is not, unfortunately, the most interesting. The ghostly bell tower over the west entrance is probably around 1000 years old, though the spire was added much later. St-Symphorian chapel contains the tomb of Saint Germanus (died 576).
✉ **Place St-Germain des Prés, 6e** Ⓜ **St-Germain des Prés** 🚌 **39, 48, 63, 70, 86,**

87, 95, 96 ⊙ Mon-Sat
8am-7.45pm, Sun 9am-
8pm ⑤ free ⟁

Église St-Séverin
(5, C4) A gem of flamboy-
ant Gothic architecture –
especially in the spiralling
stonework of the ambula-
tory – St-Séverin was built
in one of the oldest quarters of Paris between the
13th and 16th centuries.
Today it's a favourite sub-
ject of local artists.
⊠ 1 rue des Prêtres-
St-Séverin, 5e
Ⓜ St-Michel 🚌 21, 24,
27, 38, 85, 96 ⊙ Mon-
Sat 11am-7.30pm, Sun
9am-8.30pm ⑤ free ⟁

Église St-Sulpice
(5, B2) Delacroix's vivid
murals – *St Michael Killing
the Demon* and *Jacob
Wrestling the Angel* – are
highlights of this richly decorated 17th-century church
with its unusual Italianate
facade.
⊠ Place St-Sulpice, 6e
Ⓜ St-Sulpice

🚌 63, 70, 84, 86, 87, 96
⊙ 7.30am-7.30pm;
Mass with Gregorian
chant Sun 10.30am
⑤ free ⟁

Guimard Synagogue
(5, D7) While Paris has a
number of synagogues, the
one in Paris' first paved
street has a facade
designed by Art Nouveau
doyen Hector Guimard,
best known for his playful
metro entrances.
⊠ 8 rue Pavée, 4e
☎ 01 48 87 21 54
Ⓜ St-Paul 🚌 67, 69,
96, 76 ⊙ not open to
the public

Mosquée de Paris
(3, K13) An exotic slice of
the Maghreb in the heart of
the Quartier Latin, this
mosque was built in the
ornate Hispano-Moorish
style, with serene, decorated courtyards and pink-
marble fountains, plus an
African-style *salon de thé*
and *hammam* (bathhouse).
⊠ Place du Puits-de-

l'Ermite, 5e
☎ 01 45 35 97 33
Ⓜ Place Monge
🚌 63, 67, 86, 87, 89
⊙ Sat-Thurs 9am-noon,
2-6pm ⑤ donation ⟁

Mosquée de Paris: glorious
Islamic architecture

PLACES & SPACES

Place de Furstemberg
(5, A3) Tucked in behind
Église St-Germain des Prés,
this tiny little square takes
on a special life on summer
evenings, when magnolias
perfume the air and buskers
serenade lovers under the
old-fashioned streetlamp.
⊠ Place de
Furstemberg, 6e
Ⓜ St-Germain des Prés
🚌 39, 48, 63, 70, 86,
87, 95, 96

Place de l'Hôtel de
Ville (5, C6)
Since the Middle Ages this
fountain-and-lamp-

adorned square has been
the venue for many of
Paris' celebrations, rebel-
lions, book burnings and
public executions. In winter
the square is adorned by a
dinky ice-skating rink.
⊠ Place de l'Hôtel de
Ville, 1er Ⓜ Hôtel de
Ville 🚌 67, 86, 87

Place de la Bastille
(3, G15) The prison has
gone, but the mobs remain –
mostly heading to the trendy
bars and restaurants nearby.
In the centre, gilded Liberty
perches atop the **Colonne
de Juillet** (July Column), a

memorial to the revolutions
of 1830 and 1848.
⊠ Place de la Bastille,
11e Ⓜ Bastille

Place de la Concorde
(3, D7) Louis XVI was
guillotined here in 1793,
followed by another 1343
victims over the next two
years. Renamed following
the Reign of Terror, it's now
the world's most chaotic
traffic roundabout, with fab
vistas from its 3300-year-
old Egyptian obelisk.
⊠ Place de la Concorde,
8e Ⓜ Concorde 🚌 24,
42, 52, 72, 73, 84, 94

Place de la Contrescarpe (5, E3)

This convivial little square in the Quartier Latin, frequented by students, is a great place for a quick lunch or an *apéritif* before heading off to one of the dozens of inexpensive restaurants nearby.

✉ **Place de la Contrescarpe, 5e** Ⓜ **Place Monge** 🚌 47

Place des Abbesses

(4, D5) This bustling little square is a far better place to sample the 'village' life of Montmartre than tourist-trap Place du Tertre. Don't miss the original Hector Guimard Art Nouveau metro entrance, one of only two surviving.
✉ **Place des Abbesses, 18e** Ⓜ **Abbesses** 🚌 30, 31, 54, 56, 67, 80, 85, 95

Place du Marché Ste-Catherine (5, E7)

This pretty little tree-lined square, right on the edge of the Marais, is surrounded by cafes, restaurants and bars. A very peaceful and restorative spot.
✉ **Place du Marché Ste-Catherine, 4e** Ⓜ **St-Paul** 🚌 20, 29, 61, 65, 69, 76, 86, 87, 91

Place des Victoires

(3, D10) Designed for Louis XIV by the architect of Versailles, this charming and intimate 'square', surrounded by a ring of elegant 17th-century buildings, is now home to the designer labels Kenzo, Victoire and Mugler.
✉ **Place des Victoires, 1er, 2e** Ⓜ **Sentier** 🚌 29, 48, 67, 74

Place Vendôme (3, C8)

Austere, pompous and beautiful, octagonal Place Vendôme and the arcaded and colonnaded buildings around it epitomise Parisian wealth and privilege. Napoleon married Josephine at No 3, and Di and Dodi took the Merc for a final spin from the **Hôtel Ritz** (p. 102).
✉ **Place Vendôme, 1er** Ⓜ **Tuileries** 🚌 72

Cafe society, Place de la Bastille

Simon Bracken

PARKS & PROMENADES

Bois de Boulogne

(2, E2) These huge Haussmann-designed woods on the western edge of the city boast lakes, lawns, forests, flower gardens, meandering paths, cycling trails and *belle époque* cafes. Have a picnic, hire a bike or rowing boat, or stroll through the beautiful **Parc de Bagatelle** (2, D2). Kids will love the Jardin d'Acclimatation (p. 46)
Ⓜ **Porte Dauphine, Porte Maillot, Porte d'Auteuil**
🚌 43, 52, 63, 73, 82 ⏱ 24hrs (avoid after dark) ⓢ free ♿

Bois de Vincennes

(2, J15) These vast, well-ordered gardens east of the city have three lakes, a **zoo** (p. 45), floral and tropical gardens, a Buddhist centre and bike paths. The Foire du Trône amusement park (Apr-May) and turreted, medieval Château de Vincennes are also worth a look.
☎ 01 48 08 31 20
Ⓜ **Château de Vincennes** 🚊 **RER Nogent-sur-Marne** 🚌 325, 56 ⏱ park dawn-dusk; château 10am-5pm (summer to 6pm) ⓢ park free; château €5.50/4 ♿

Canal St-Martin

(2, D11) The 4.5km-long Canal St-Martin is one of Paris' hidden delights. Its shaded towpaths – dappled with sunlight filtering through the plane trees – are a wonderful place for a romantic stroll or bike ride past nine locks, lovely bridges and ordinary Parisian neighbourhoods.
Ⓜ **République, Jaurès, Stalingrad**

Cimetière du Montparnasse (3, K8)

This tranquil little cemetery contains the tombs of such illustrious personages as Charles Baudelaire, Samuel

Beckett, Guy de Maupassant, Simone de Beauvoir and Jean-Paul Sartre, André Citroën, Alfred Dreyfus, Jean Seberg, Serge Gainsbourg and Man Ray. Don't miss Constantin Brancusi's intriguing sculpture *The Kiss*.

✉ **Conservation office, 3 blvd Edgar Quinet, 14e** ☎ **01 44 10 86 50** Ⓜ **Edgar Quinet, Raspail** 🚌 **54, 80, 95, 320** ◷ **Mon-Fri 8am-6pm (winter to 5.30pm), Sat from 8.30am, Sun from 9am** Ⓢ **free** ♿ **limited**

Jardin des Plantes

(3, J14) Founded in 1626 as a medicinal herb garden for Louis XIII, Paris' botanical gardens are endearingly informal, even unkempt. There are several greenhouses, a small *ménagerie* and the fascinating **Grande Galerie de l'Evolution**, (part of the Musée National d'Histoire Naturelle).

✉ **57 rue Cuvier, 5e** ☎ **01 40 79 30 00** e **www.mnhn.fr** Ⓜ **Gare d'Austerlitz, Jussieu** 🚌 **24, 61, 63, 65, 67, 89, 91** ◷ **park dawn-dusk; galerie Mon & Wed-Fri 10am-5pm (6pm Summer weekends)** Ⓢ **galerie €4.60/3.05** ♿ **limited**

Jardin des Tuileries

(3, D8) Once the most fashionable strolling park in Paris, the formal Tuileries offers rest from the crowds, plus great views. Kids can float boats in the pond, and twice a year there's a carnival with heart-stopping Ferris-wheel rides.

☎ **01 40 20 90 43** Ⓜ **Tuileries, Concorde** 🚌 **21, 27, 39, 48, 68, 69, 72, 81, 95** ◷ **dawn-dusk** Ⓢ **free** ♿

New Wine from Old Barrels

The former wine warehousing quarter of Bercy, on the Seine at the eastern end of Paris, is now the site of an ambitious urban renewal project. The warehouses themselves (dating from 1877) have been converted into **Bercy Village** (2, J12; Ⓜ Cour St-Émilion), a kind of outdoor shopping mall, with bars and restaurants, and a huge cinema complex nearby. The **Marina de Bercy** and **Sable en Seine** (Sand on the Seine – a kind of seasonal beach) are helping to reclaim this reach of the river, as are the *péniches* (barges) moored nearby – home to more bars, restaurants and clubs.

Adjacent **Parc de Bercy** is a pleasant green space for a stroll. A fun way to get there is to take the driverless Météor (metro line 14) to the Bibliothèque terminus and walk across the Pont de Tolbiac.

Parc André Citroën

(2, H4) Built on the banks of the Seine on the 14-hectare former Citroën manufacturing plant, this high-tech architect-designed park is a series of thematic 'spaces' – the 'white garden', the 'black garden' and the whimsical 'restless garden'.

✉ **rue Balard, 15e** Ⓜ **Balard** 🚌 **42** ◷ **dawn-dusk** ♿

Parc de Monceau

(2, C7) The dauntingly pretty Parc de Monceau is surrounded by the chic and expensive apartments of the *haute bourgeoisie*, and has immaculately tended lawns, pseudo-classical statuary and the city's best-dressed kids out with their nannies.

✉ **blvd de Courcelles, 8e** Ⓜ **Monceau** 🚌 **30, 84, 94** ◷ **dawn-dusk** ♿

Parc des Buttes Chaumont

(2, C13) A slice of Manhattan's Central Park in the northeast of Paris, this former quarry is now a lush, hilly landscape with a huge lake, forested slopes, hidden grottoes, artificial waterfalls and views of Montmartre. A good spot for jogging, tanning or listening to birds.

✉ **rue Armand Carrel, 19e** ☎ **01 40 36 41 32** Ⓜ **Buttes Chaumont, Botzaris** 🚌 **26, 60, 75** ◷ **7am-9pm (summer to 11pm)** Ⓢ **free** ♿ **limited**

Promenade Plantée

(2, G12) For an elevated perspective over eastern Paris, follow the tree and flower-lined *coulée verte* (green strip) built atop the 4.5km **Viaduc des Arts** that once carried trains between Bastille and the Bois de Vincennes. Below are the trendy shops and *ateliers* of the viaduct.

✉ **av Daumesnil between Opéra Bastille and Porte Dorée, 12e** e **www.promenade-plantee.org** Ⓜ **Bastille, Reuilly Diderot**

QUIRKY PARIS

Catacombes de Paris

(2, H9) From 1785, nearly 6 million skeletons were taken from Paris' overburdened cemeteries and stacked neatly in disused underground quarries, creating Paris' most macabre museum. The Résistance used the tunnels as a WWII HQ.

✉ **1 Place Denfert Rochereau, 14e**
☎ **01 43 22 47 63**
Ⓜ **Denfert Rochereau**
🚌 **38, 68** ⊘ **Tues 11am-4pm, Wed-Sun 9am-4pm** ⑤ **€5/3.35**

Colette's Water Bar

(3, D8) Sick of nursing a *gueule de bois* (hangover) the next day? At the 'water bar' in the basement of this chic shopping temple you can tipple 100 types of drinking water – both sparkling and still – from around the world.

✉ **213 rue St-Honoré, 1er** ☎ **01 55 35 33 90**
ℯ **www.colette.tm.fr**
Ⓜ **Tuileries, Pyramides**
🚌 **68, 72** ⊘ **10.30am-7.30pm** ♿ **limited**

Deyrolle (3, F8)

This fusty, olde-worlde shoppe is stuffed with things that are, well, stuffed. Taxidermists serving the rich and loony since 1831 (many of the specimens obviously date from the early days), they will even future-proof your own moggy or pooch (or polar bear for that matter).

✉ **46 rue du Bac, 7e**
☎ **01 42 22 30 07**
Ⓜ **Rue du Bac** 🚌 **63, 69, 84, 94** ⊘ **Mon-Sat 10am-7.30pm**

Galerie de la SEITA

(3, 5E) Seita, the state-run tobacco company, sponsors this fascinating little museum on the history of tobacco usage and its fetishes. No smoking allowed!

✉ **12 rue Surcouf, 8e**
☎ **01 45 56 60 17**
Ⓜ **Invalides** 🚌 **28, 49, 63** ⊘ **11am-7pm**
⑤ **€4/2.50**

Musée de l'Érotisme

(4, D3) Pigalle's Museum of Eroticism tries to put titillating statuary and sexual aids from days gone by on a loftier plane – with seven floors of erotic art from four continents. But we all know why we've come.

✉ **72 blvd de Clichy, 18e** ☎ **01 42 58 28 73**
ℯ **www.erotic-museum.com**

Blanche

Ⓜ **Blanche** 🚌 **30, 54**
⊘ **10am-2am**
⑤ **€6.10/4.60** ♿ **limited**

Musée des Égouts de Paris (3, D4)

Raw sewage (complete with all sorts of vaguely familiar floating objects) flows beneath your feet as you walk through 480m (of more than 2100km!) of odoriferous tunnels, passing artefacts illustrating the development of Paris' wastewater disposal system.

✉ **93 Quai d'Orsay, 7e**
☎ **01 53 68 27 81**
Ⓜ **Alma-Marceau**
🚌 **42, 63, 80, 92**
⊘ **Sat-Wed 11am-5pm (summer), 11am-4pm (winter)** ⑤ **€3.80/2.30**

Musée de l'Érotisme covers eroticism from top to bottom

PARIS FOR CHILDREN

Children's Gallery – Centre Pompidou

(3, E12) Innovative and engaging workshops and exhibitions where children can get their hands dirty trying out modern art and performance.

✉ Centre Pompidou, rue St-Martin, 4e
☎ 01 44 78 49 13
e www.centrepomp idou.fr ⓜ Rambuteau
🚌 21, 29, 38, 47, 58, 69, 70, 72, 74, 75, 76, 81, 85, 96
🕐 workshops Wed & Sat afternoon; exhibition Wed-Mon 1-7pm
$ €8 ⓗ limited

Jardin d'Acclimatation

(2, C3) This park, funfair and amusement park for the youngsters in the Bois de Boulogne has puppet shows, an enchanted-river boat ride, a toy train, dodgems, mini-golf, donkey rides and a children's zoo.

✉ Bois de Boulogne, 16e ☎ 01 40 67 90 82
ⓜ Les Sablons
🚌 43, 52, 63, 73, 82
🕐 10am-7pm
(10.30pm Summer Fri)
$ €1.50 for some attractions ⓗ limited

Le Musée de la Poupée

(5, B8) A delightful little museum with more than 300 dolls (many of French porcelain) from 1840 to today, together with doll houses, accessories, miniature toys, and a doll hospital and shop.

✉ Impasse Berthaud (nr 22 rue Beaubourg), 3e ☎ 01 42 72 73 11
ⓜ Rambuteau
🚌 29, 38, 47, 75
🕐 Tues-Sun 10am-6pm
$ €5.35/3.80 ⓗ

Babysitting

For a current listing of babysitting services, try **Inter-service Parents** (☎ 01 44 93 44 93). **Ababa** (☎ 01 45 49 46 46) is a recommended service: €4.75/hr plus agency fees of €10, plus taxi fare after 11pm. Similar is **Kid Services** (☎ 01 42 61 90 00; e www .kidservices.fr). English-speaking students are sometimes available for child minding through **Alliance Française** (☎ 01 42 84 90 00).

Sandpit at Place des Vosges

Rob Flynn

Musée Grévin (3, B10)

This recently refurbished waxworks museum is located in a wonderful building in the Passage Jouffroy. Includes plenty of recognisable characters as well as some French favourites. There's also a Magic Theatre and Hall of Mirrors from 1900.

✉ Passage Jouffroy, 10-12 blvd Montmartre, 9e ☎ 01 47 70 85 05
e www.musee-grevin .com ⓜ Grands-Boulevards 🚌 20, 48, 74, 85 🕐 10am-7pm
$ €15/9.15 ⓗ limited

Palais de la Découverte (3, D5)

Tucked away in the Grand Palais, and usually full of earnest school groups, the Palace of Discovery has informative interactive exhibits on the sciences, from astronomy (including a state-of-the-art planetarium) to medicine.

✉ av Franklin D Roosevelt, 8e
☎ 01 56 43 20 21
e www.palais-decou verte.fr ⓜ Champs Élysées Clemenceau
🚌 28, 42, 49, 52, 63, 72, 73, 80, 83, 93
🕐 Tues-Sat 9.30am-6pm, Sun 10am-7pm; planetarium 11.30am, 2.15, 3.30 & 4.45pm
$ €5.65/3.70/12.20; planetarium +€3.05 ⓗ limited

Parc Astérix (1, A8)
A home-grown alternative to Disneyland with 'regions' to explore (Village of the Gauls, Roman Empire, Ancient Greece etc), rides to avoid (Zeus Thunder, Oxygenarium flume), and a Dolphinarium. There's also six restaurants and 40 fast-food outlets!
✉ 36km from Paris, near Roissy airport
☎ 03 44 62 34 34
e www.parcasterix.fr
🚆 RER line B3 from

Châtelet or Gare du Nord to Roissy CDG 1, then shuttle bus (every 30mins 9am-2pm)
◷ Apr-Oct only: 10am-6pm Mon-Fri, 9.30am-7pm Sat-Sun & daily mid-July-Aug; check as hrs vary ⑤ €28.20/20.60 ♿ limited

Parc Zoologique de Paris (2, J15)
The 1200 captives in France's largest zoo include all the usual exotic

suspects, plus panda; the wild mountain sheep who live on the 70m-high artificial rock in the centre of the park seem to have the most fun. Summer weekends are usually crowded.
✉ 53 av St-Maurice, 12e ☎ 01 44 75 20 10
e www.mnhn.fr
Ⓜ Porte Dorée
🚌 46, 325 ◷ summer 9am-6pm (Sun to 6.30pm); closes 1hr earlier winter
⑤ €7.65/4.60/1.50 ♿

KEEPING FIT

It's not unusual to gain an extra kilo or two during a visit to Paris, no matter how many museum corridors you pound. **Allô-Sports** (☎ 08 20 00 75 75) is a useful helpline (English spoken) offering advice on sports and activities throughout Paris.

Aquaboulevard (2, J4)
Huge recreational centre offering a range of activities for adults and kids, including swimming pool, 'beach' and aquatic park, tennis, squash, golf practice and gym, restaurants etc.
✉ 4 rue Louis-Armand, 15e ☎ 01 40 60 10 00
Ⓜ Balard ◷ Mon-Fri 9am-11pm (midnight Fri); Sat-Sun 8am-11pm (midnight Sat) ⑤ €18.30/9.15 half-day entry

Bains du Marais (5, C7)
Comfortable, modern bath complex offering a smorgasbord of treatments including traditional Moroccan glove massage (gommage), essential oil massage, shampoo, facial, pedicure and henna tattoos.
✉ 31-33 rue des Blancs Manteaux, 4e ☎ 01 44 61 02 02
e www.lesbainsdu marais.com Ⓜ Hotel-de-Ville 🚌 47, 58, 69,

70, 72, 74, 96
◷ women: 11am-8pm Mon, 11am-11pm Tues, 10am-7pm Wed; men: 11am-11pm Thurs, 10am-8pm Fri-Sat; mixed: 7pm-midnight Wed, 11am-11pm Sun
⑤ hammam: €28, massage €28/30mins

Chez Nickel (3, B8)
Men are à la mode in Paris, and this swish new salon in the basement of Printemps department store will ensure your beau mec (good lookin' guy) is trimmed, waxed, shaven, tanned, massaged and lotioned within an inch of his life.
✉ Printemps de l'Homme, 64 blvd Hausmann, 9e ☎ 01 42 82 64 75 e www.printem ps.fr Ⓜ Havre-Caumartin 🚌 20, 21, 24, 27, 29, 53, 66 ◷ Mon-Sat 10am-7pm (10pm Thurs) ⑤ waxing €15-50; massage €13

Jogging
You rarely see joggers in Paris because of the pollution and traffic. And then there's the style police who frown on sweaty people in shorts. Best spots for an uninterrupted run are the **Champ de Mars** (2, F6), **Jardin du Luxembourg** (2, G9), **Parc des Buttes Chaumont** (2, C12) or along the **Promenade Plantée** (2, G12). Try the **Bois de Boulogne** (2, E2) and **Bois de Vincennes** (2, J15) further afield.

Dojo Zen de Paris
(2, J10) Perhaps not an activity to open up the sweat pores, but a session of zazen just might open your third eye. The dojo was founded by Taisen

Deshimaru in 1971; free introductory zazen sessions are offered Sat at 4pm.
✉ **175 rue de Tolbiac, 13e** ☎ **01 53 80 19 19** Ⓜ **Tolbiac** 🚌 **47, 62** ⏰ zazen Tues-Fri 6.30 & 7.30am, 12.30 & 7pm, Sat 11am & 5pm, Sun 11am ⑤ €6 per session, €35 per month

Gymnase Club (3, E9)
Paris' biggest chain of gyms has over 20 locations in the city and good facilities (some including pools and sauna).
✉ **147bis rue St-Honoré, 1er** ☎ **01 44 37 24 24** **e** **www.gymnaseclub.fr** Ⓜ **Palais-Royal** ⏰ ⑤ depends on location

Gymnasium (3, E12)
Over 25 locations throughout Paris, with aerobics and some with pools and sauna.
✉ **62 blvd de Sébastopol, 3e** ☎ **01 42 74 14 56** **e** **www.gymnasium.fr** Ⓜ **Etienne Marcel** ⏰ **Mon-Fri 7.30am-10pm, Sat 9am-7pm, Sun 9am-5pm** ⑤ depends on location

Hammam de la Mosquée de Paris (3, K13) Step out of the west and into the east in this wonderfully exotic bathhouse at Paris' Grand Mosque. Relax in the public baths (men and women on different days) or experience a traditional massage. Finish with mint tea.
✉ **39 rue Geoffroy-St-Hilaire, 5e** ☎ **01 43 31 18 14** Ⓜ **Place Monge** 🚌 **67, 89** ⏰ **10am-9pm; men Tues & Sun, women other days** ⑤ baths €14; massage €9.50 ♿ limited

Cycling
Paris traffic is dangerous, so don't even think of renting a bike unless you're a confident big-city cyclist. Two of the best city rides away from the traffic along the-closed-to-traffic **river** quais (between Bercy and Pond de l'Alama) on Sunday, and along the 50km **Canal St-Martin/Canal de l'Ourcq** route – traffic-free after Place de la Bataille de Stalingrad (2, C11). Otherwise, head for the relative safety of the **Bois du Boulogne** and **Bois de Vincennes**. Paris à Vélo c'est Sympa (see Bicycle Tours, p. 54) rents bikes and offers interesting bike tours.

Martin Moos

Pari Roller (3, K7)
Every Friday night more than 5000 skaters (record 28,000!) take to the streets for an officially sponsored 3hr, 25km frolic through the heart of the city.
✉ **departs from in front of Gare Montparnasse, 14e** **e** **www.pari-roller .com** Ⓜ **Montparnasse Bienvenüe** ⏰ **Fri 10pm-1am** ⑤ free

Piscine Pontoise (5, E5)
Beautiful Art Deco-style swimming pool (33m) in the heart of the Quartier Latin. Complex also includes gym and squash courts.
✉ **19 rue de Pontoise, 5e** ☎ **01 55 42 77 88**

Ⓜ **Maubert-Mutualité** 🚌 **47, 63, 86** ⏰ check hours: Mon-Fri 7-8.30am, 12.15-1.30pm & 4.30-8.45pm (7.15pm Thurs); Sun 10am-7pm ⑤ €4.30/3.80

Piscine Suzanne Berlioux (5, A7)
A 50m swimming pool, surrounded by a tropical garden inside Paris' largest shopping mall. Busy, but fun.
✉ **Forum des Halles, 1er** ☎ **01 42 36 98 44** Ⓜ **Les Halles** ⏰ **Mon-Fri 11.30am-9.30pm, Sat-Sun 9am-6.30pm** ⑤ €4.60/3.80

out & about

WALKING TOURS
Serene Seine Stroll

The secret of this lovely walk is to savour the view from each bridge. Cross Pont Marie ❶ to charming Île St-Louis, browsing in the boutiques and taking the stairs to the eastern tip of the island.

Sample a Berthillon ice cream ❷ as you cross Pont St-Louis to the Île de la Cité. Visit the Mémorial des Martyrs de la Déportation ❸ then wander through Square Jean XXIII ❹ for a close encounter with Notre Dame ❺. Follow Quai aux Fleurs through the flower markets ❻ to the Tour de l'Horloge and the Conciergerie ❼. Pass the Palais de Justice and Sainte Chapelle ❽, and take Quai des Orfèvres to secluded Place Dauphine ❾.

Cross Pont Neuf to picnic in the Square du Vert Galant ❿, overlooked by the statue of Henri IV.

Wave to the passing boats from the Pont des Arts ⓫ before heading through the Cour Carrée of the Musée du Louvre ⓬ to the glass pyramid ⓭. Pass under the Arc de Triomphe du Carrousel ⓮ to reach the Jardin des Tuileries ⓯.

Stroll through the gardens to emerge at Pont de la Concorde ⓰. Pass Pont Alexandre III ⓱, the Diana memorial ⓲ and the Jardins du Trocadéro ⓳, and finish the walk with a fabulous view of the Tour Eiffel ⓴.

Simon Bracken

Gothically gorgeous Notre Dame

distance 7km **duration** 3hrs
▶ **start** Ⓜ Pont Marie
● **end** Ⓜ Trocadéro

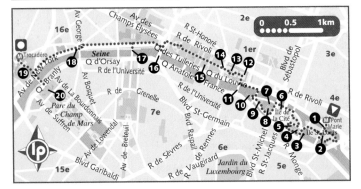

Marvellous Marais Ramble

From BHV department store **1**, saunter along cafe-lined rue des Archives. Turn right at the Archives Nationales **2**, left past the Hôtel de Rohan **3** and right until Place de Thorigny. Visit the Musée Picasso **4** or Musée de la Serrure-Bricard **5**, or continue to lovely Square Léopold Achille **6** or Square Georges Cain **7** for a picnic.

Turn left into rue des Francs Bourgeois, passing the Musée Carnavalet **8**, to reach the impressive Place des Vosges **9**.

A door in the south-west corner leads through the Hôtel de Sully **10** to bustling rue St-Antoine. Turn right, and after a detour to Place du Marché Ste-Catherine **11**, turn right again into rue Pavée for the Guimard Synagogue **12**. Turn left into rue des Rosiers, the heart of the Jewish quarter for a kosher felafel at Chez Marianne **13**.

Left into rue Vieille du Temple takes you across rue de Rivoli.

SIGHTS & HIGHLIGHTS

Musée Picasso (p. 26)
Musée de la Serrure-Bricard (p. 37)
Musée Carnavalet (p. 36)
Place des Vosges (p. 30)
Place du Marché Ste-Catherine (p. 42)
Hôtel de Sully (p. 39)
Guimard Synagogue (p. 41)
Chez Marianne (p. 77)
Musée de la Curiosité et de la Magie (p. 36)

Rob Flynn

Hotel de Ville

Spicy rue François Miron, rue de Jouy and rue de l'Ave Maria lead to the Hôtel de Sens **14**. Learn a trick or two at the Musée de la Curiosité et de la Magie **15** or browse antiques in Village St-Paul. Follow ancient rue Charlemagne to glimpse a remnant of the 12th-century city wall **16**. The walk ends at the St-Paul metro via tiny rue du Prévôt.

distance 3.5km **duration** 2½hrs
▶ **start** Ⓜ Hôtel de Ville
● **end** Ⓜ St-Paul

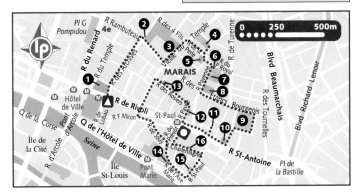

Left Bank Loop

From Fontaine St-Michel ❶ cross blvd St-Michel and meander through the streets around rue de la Huchette and Église St-Séverin ❷. Cross the road to Église St-Julien-le-Pauvre and Square Viviani ❸, and browse through the books at Shakespeare and Company ❹.

Follow the *quais*, turning right into rue des Fossés St-Bernard, passing the Institut du Monde Arabe ❺. Left into rue Jussieu then right into rue Linné brings you to the Roman Arènes de Lutèce ❻. Going down hill, stroll through the Jardin des Plantes ❼ or stop for mint tea at the Mosquée de Paris ❽.

Rue Daubenton leads to funky rue Mouffetard ❾. Wind your way up the narrow market street, noting George Orwell's former down-and-out digs at 6 rue Pot-de-Fer ❿, and grab a bite at La Chope Café in Place de la Contrescarpe ⓫. Ernest Hemingway once lived at 74 rue du Cardinal Lemoine ⓬. Continue along rue Descartes, turning left into rue Clovis for Église St-Étienne du Mont ⓭ and the Panthéon ⓮.

Follow rue Soufflot, with the Sorbonne ⓯ on your right, to the Jardin du Luxembourg ⓰. Cobbled rue Servandoni leads to massive Église St-Sulpice ⓱ and the chic shopping *quartier* around Place du Quebec ⓲. Cross blvd St-Germain to the Église St-Germain des Prés ⓳, with the famous cafes Deux Magots and Café de Flore ⓴ to your left. Behind the church, visit pretty Place de Furstemberg ㉑ before taking bustling rue de Buci and rue St-André des Arts back to St-Michel.

distance 6km **duration** 3hrs
▶ **start** Ⓜ St-Michel
● **end** Ⓜ St-Michel

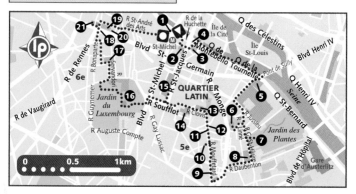

Montmartre Art Attack

Stride past saucy Moulin Rouge and Musée de l'Érotisme ❶ up shop-lined rue Lepic. Detour left at rue des Abbesses to visit the Cimetière de Montmartre ❷ then return to rue Lepic to see van Gogh's home (3rd floor, No 54) ❸.

Climb rue Tholozé until you regain rue Lepic, with its two evocative windmills ❹ & ❺. Turn left into rue Girardon, cross Square St-Buisson ❻ and veer right through charming Allée des Brouillards (Fog Alley) ❼.

SIGHTS & HIGHLIGHTS

Musée de l'Érotisme (p. 44)
Le Lapin Agile (p. 93)
Basilique du Sacré Cœur (p. 31)
Espace Montmartre Salvador Dalí (p. 37)
Place des Abbesses (p. 42)

Descend the stairs from Place Dalida into rue St-Vincent, passing the Cimetière St-Vincent ❽. Turn right at the bohemian Lapin Agile ❾ and past the vineyard ❿. Turn left into rue Cortot, passing Montmartre's oldest house (now the Musée de Montmartre) ⓫ and Eric Satie's house at No 6 ⓬.

Turn right at the water tower ⓭ and left to reach Sacré Cœur ⓮

Easel does it in Montmartre

for a stunning vista over Paris. Walk past the funicular station and ancient St-Pierre de Montmartre ⓯ to touristy Place du Tertre ⓰.

Follow rue Poulbot past the Dalí museum ⓱. Descend the steps from Place du Calvaire ⓲ into rue Gabrielle, turning right to reach Place Émile Goudeau ⓳ and, at No 13, the rebuilt Bateau Lavoir studio where Picasso & Co set up their easels. Take the steps and turn left at rue des Abbesses to reach the Guimard-designed metro station at Place des Abbesses ⓴.

distance 2.5km **duration** 2hrs
▶ **start** Ⓜ Blanche
● **end** Ⓜ Abbesses

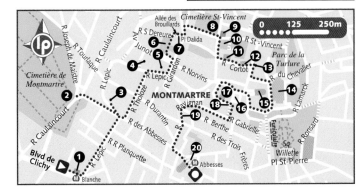

EXCURSIONS

Château de Fontainebleau (1, E9)

If you must see one French chateau, make it the enormous 1900-room Château de Fontainebleau, whose list of former tenants reads like a who's who of French royal history. It is one of the most beautifully decorated and furnished chateaux in France, with every centimetre of wall and ceiling space richly adorned with wood panelling, gilded carvings, frescoes, tapestries and paintings.

In addition to the magnificent apartments, and courtyards, the **Musée Napoleon 1er** has person-

INFORMATION

65km south-east of Paris
- 🚊 Gare de Lyon to Fontainebleau-Avon (40-60mins; €7.35)
- ☎ 01 60 71 50 70
- 🌐 www.fontainebleau.org
- ℹ️ Fontainebleau tourist office (☎ 01 60 74 99 99, 4 rue Royale)
- 🕐 Wed-Mon: June-Sept 9.30am-6pm; Oct-May 9.30am-5pm
- 💲 €5.35/3.50; Sun €3.50

al effects belonging to Napoleon, the **Musée Chinois** is filled with exquisite pieces from Asia, and there are several beautiful gardens and an adjacent forest to stroll in.

A Château view across the lake

Cathédrale de Chartres (1, E4)

The magnificent 13th-century Notre Dame de Chartres, dominating the medieval town from which it rises, is one of the crowning architectural achievements of western civilisation. The cathedral's astonishing original stained-glass windows (renowned for their intense blue tones), ornamented portals and two soaring spires – one Gothic, the other Romanesque – make it a must-do day trip from Paris.

The cathedral's collection of relics – particularly the **Sainte Chemise**, said to have been worn by the Virgin Mary when she gave birth to Jesus – attracted pilgrims during the Middle Ages.

The adjacent **Musée des Beaux-Arts** (☎ 02 37 36 41 39, 29 Cloître Notre-Dame) has some outstanding pieces from the 16-19th centuries.

INFORMATION

90km south-west of Paris
- 🚊 Gare Montparnasse to Chartres
- ☎ 02 37 21 56 33
- ℹ️ tourist office (☎ 02 37 21 50 00, Place de la Cathédrale)
- 🕐 cathedral: winter 8.30am-7.30pm, summer 7.30am-8pm; museum Wed-Mon 10am-noon & 2-5pm, Apr-Oct to 6pm
- 💲 cathedral & treasury free; Clocher Neuf (New Bell Tower) €3.80/2.30 (free under 12); museum €2.40/1.20; tours in English: (☎ 02 37 28 15 58) Mon-Sat noon & 2.45pm €6.10/3.05; crypte €2.40/1.20; museum €3.20/1.60

Disneyland Paris (1, B9)

Disneyland Paris is the most popular fee-paying attraction in Europe, welcoming more than 100 million 'guests' since it opened in 1992. It consists of three main areas: Disneyland Park, Walt Disney Studios (due to open Spring 2002) and the commercial Disneyland Village.

Disneyland Park is the focus: a replica of Disney amusement parks in the USA and Japan, with five *pays* (lands) to explore: Main Street USA, Frontierland, Adventureland, Fantasyland and Discoveryland. There's all the Disney characters plus plenty of thrilling rides like the Indiana Jones and the Temple of Doom roller coaster, Space Mountain and Orbitron (don't even ask!).

Disney Studios will be both a

> ## INFORMATION
>
> ### 32km east of Paris
> - 🚊 RER line A4 to Marne-la-Vallée-Chessy (35-40mins; €5.80/2.90)
> - ☎ 01 60 30 60 30; 0870 503 03 03 in the UK; 407-WDISNEY in the US
> - **e** www.disneylandparis.com
> - ⏱ Sept-June 10am-6pm, July-Aug 9am-11pm (variable according to day; call ahead to check)
> - 💲 one-day 'passport' €35.98/28.05 Apr-Nov & Christmas, €27/23 Nov-Mar; multi-day tickets also available

working film-production studio as well as film theme park. **Disneyland Village** has a 15-screen cinema, shops, restaurants, bars and even a skating rink. The complex also has seven hotels, 61 food and drink outlets, 56 shops and a 27-hole golf course.

Musée Claude Monet – Giverny (1, A4)

The small village of Giverny was the home of Impressionist Claude Monet from 1883-1926 and where he painted some of his most famous works, including *Décorations des Nymphéas* (Water Lilies). Here you'll find his famous pastel pink-and-green house, Water Lily studio and flower-filled gardens.

Giverny's gardens reflect the seasons. From early to late spring, daffodils, tulips, rhododendrons and irises appear, followed by poppies and lilies. By June, nasturtiums, roses and sweet pea are in flower. Around September, there are dahlias, sunflowers and hollyhocks. And, of course, the wisteria-clad Japanese bridge, the pond and water lilies.

Nearby is the **Musée Américain** (☎ 02 32 51 94 65; €5.35/3.05) containing the works of many American Impressionists.

> ## INFORMATION
>
> ### 76km west of Paris
> - 🚊 Gare St-Lazare to Vernon, then bus
> - ☎ 02 32 51 28 21
> - ⏱ Apr-Oct Tues-Sun 10am-6pm
> - 💲 €5.35/3.80/3.05

Christopher Wood

Monet's inspirational home at Giverny

ORGANISED TOURS

You'll find a wide variety of tours (mostly in French) advertised in *L'Officiel des Spectacles* and *Pariscope*, under the headings *promenades* or *conférences*.

BICYCLE TOURS

Paris à Vélo c'est Sympa (3, G15)
Michel Nöe offers a range of interesting (even quirky) half-day thematic bike tours (English spoken) covering central and outer Paris, as well as dawn, night and full-day (summer) excursions.
✉ 37 blvd Bourdon, 4e
☎ 01 48 87 60 01
e www.parisvelosympa
.com ⏰ Mon-Fri 9am-1pm & 2-6pm; Sat-Sun 9am-6pm
💲 €28/24.40; deposit €610 (credit card)

Paris Vélo (3, K13)
Well-organised bilingual tours of major sightseeing areas such as the Marais, Île St-Louis and Quartier Latin, plus an ad-libbed night tour.
☎ 01 43 37 59 22
e www.paris-velo-rent-a-bike.fr
💲 €27.45/18.30 half-day

DIY River Tour

From April to October the **Batobus** river shuttle (☎ 01 44 11 33 99; e www.batobus.com) runs every 25mins 10am-7pm (Jul-Aug to 9pm). Tickets start at €3.05/1.55 per stop or €9.90/5.35 for a day pass. Jump aboard at:
- Tour Eiffel
- Musée d'Orsay
- St-Germain des Prés
- Notre Dame
- Hôtel de Ville
- Musée du Louvre

BOAT TOURS

Bateaux Mouches (3, D4) Bateaux Mouches runs the biggest tour boats on the Seine. Cruises depart/return Pont de l'Alma, and pass the Statue of Liberty and Tour Eiffel in the west, and Île St-Louis in the east; cruises last 1¼hrs.
✉ Pont de l'Alma, 8e
☎ 01 42 25 96 10; English recording 01 40 76 99 99
e www.bateauxm ouches.com ⏰ summer every 30mins 10am-8pm, every 20mins 8-11pm; winter 11am, 2.30, 4, 6 & 9pm
💲 €6.85/3.05; €45.75 lunch; €83.85 dinner (smart dress)

Bateaux Parisiens (3, E2) One-hour Seine cruises with commentary in multiple languages. The 2hr lunch/3hr dinner cruises include meals and wine.
✉ Port de la Bourdonnais, 7e
☎ 01 44 11 33 55
e www.bateauxp arisiens.com ⏰ Easter-Oct every 30mins 10am-10.30pm; Nov-Easter every hr 10am-9pm 💲 €8.40/4.15; €45.75-68.60 lunch; €88.40-118 dinner

Canauxrama (3, G15) Three-hour cruises along charming Canal St-Martin and Canal de l'Ourcq between Port de l'Arsenal and Parc de la Villette.
✉ Port de l'Arsenal, opp 50 blvd de la Bastille, 12e; Bassin de la Villette, 13 Quai de la Loire, 19e
☎ 01 42 39 15 00
e www.canauxrama .com ⏰ From Parc de la Villette 9.45am & 2.45pm; from Port de l'Arsenal 9.45am & 2.30pm 💲 Mon-Fri €10.70/9.90/7.65; Sat-Sun €10.70

Paris Canal Croisières (2, B13) Three-hour cruise along the Seine and canals from the Musée d'Orsay to Parc de la Villette. Reservations required.
✉ Quai Anatole France (3, E7) or Parc de la Villette ☎ 01 42 40 96 97
e www.pariscanals.com ⏰ late Mar-mid-Nov depart Musée d'Orsay 9.30am, return Parc de la Villette 2.30pm (July-Aug also 2.35pm & 6.15pm)
💲 €15.25/11.45/7.65

Vedettes du Pont Neuf (5, A5)
One-hour boat excursions and lunch and dinner cruises.
✉ sq du Vert Galant, Île de la Cité, 1er
☎ 01 46 33 98 38
⏰ summer: every 30mins 10am-noon, 1.30-6.30pm & 9-10.30pm; winter: 3/day Mon-Thurs, 7/day Fri-Sun
💲 €8.40/6.85; lunch €45.75/22.85; dinner €70/53.50

BUS TOURS

Cityrama (3, D9)
Cityrama runs 2hr city tours (multi-language taped commentary) and night city tours in high-tech buses

with panoramic windows, and also offers a range of excursions further afield. Reservations unnecessary.

✉ **meet at 4 place des Pyramides** ☎ **01 44 55 61 00** e **www.cityrama.com** Ⓢ **€22.90**

Paris l'Open Tour

(3, B7) Open-topped London-style double-decker buses travel a 2¼hr circuit that takes in Notre Dame, the Tour Eiffel and Musée d'Orsay as well as the usual list of Right Bank tourist sights. Hop on or hop off the buses wherever you like over two days; commentary in English and French.

✉ **meet at Place de la Madeleine, 8e** ☎ **01 42 66 56 56** ⏰ **9.45am-6.05pm** Ⓢ **€25.95/12.20 2-day pass**

OTHER TOURS

Paristoric (3, B8)

Audiovisual presentation of Paris' 2000-year history. Designed mainly for kids, but even the oldies will learn a thing or two. Headset commentary in choice of language.

✉ **11bis rue Scribe, 9e** ☎ **01 42 66 62 06** e **www.paristoric.com** ⏰ **Apr-Oct 9am-8pm, Nov-Mar 9am-6pm** Ⓢ **€7.65/4.60/3.05**

Vélo Taxi (3, B8)

Bilingual students pedal

bright yellow cycle-rickshaws for a 1hr tour of the sights around Place de la Concorde. Departing from the Tuileries gate (3, D7), the tours pass La Madeleine, Opéra, Place Vendôme, the Musée d'Orsay and the Louvre.

✉ **12 rue Vignon, 9e** ☎ **01 42 72 70 12** ⏰ **Apr-Oct 10am-6pm** Ⓢ **€15/20 (1/2 passengers)**

WALKING TOURS

Paris Contact

Jill Daneels runs customised tours and personalised guided walks, including Montmartre, the Marais, themed walks etc. Reserve 48 hours ahead. Meeting points advised on reservation.

✉ **46 rue Lepic, 18e** ☎ **01 42 51 08 40** e **camecaUSA@aol.com** Ⓢ **from €9 per person**

Paris Walking Tours

(1, B7) Peter and Oriel Caine and their small English-speaking team offer 2hr daily walks through Paris, including Montmartre, the Marais, the Latin Quarter and the Paris of Hemingway. Meeting points advised on reservation.

✉ **12 Passage Meunier, 93200 Saint Denis** ☎ **01 48 09 21 40** e **www.paris-walks.com** Ⓢ **€10; student reductions**

DIY Bus Tours

With a little ingenuity, and for the cost of a transit ticket, you can devise your own tour on an RATP bus. Bus No 29 has an open-air platform and is a cheap, fun way to see Paris.

Bus Nos 21 or 27
Opéra, Palais Royal, Louvre, Pont Neuf, Jardin du Luxembourg, Panthéon

Bus No 29
Opéra, Centre Pompidou, Marais, Place des Vosges, Bastille, Gare de Lyon

Bus No 47
Centre Pompidou, Notre Dame, Arènes de Lutèce, Gobelins

Bus No 63
Musée d'Orsay, Trocadéro, Concorde, Invalides

Bus No 73
Concorde, Champs Élysées, Arc de Triomphe

Bus No 82
Montparnasse, Invalides, Tour Eiffel

Urban Safari

Fun do-it-yourself adventures through Paris, led by a series of text messages on your GSM mobile phone. Choose from a number of themes including chocolate, techno, art and cigars, and meet similarly wacky people on the way. A modicum of French necessary.

✉ **16 rue Euler, 8e** ☎ **01 49 52 07 25** e **www.urban-safari.com; info@urban-safari.com**

All aboard! Rise above the hustle and bustle.

shopping

Paris is a sublime place to shop, whether you're someone who can afford an original Cartier diamond bracelet or you're just an impecunious *lèche-vitrine* (window licker). From the ultra-chic couture houses to the boutiques of the Marais, Paris is a city that knows how to make it, how to present it – and how to charge for it.

Unlike many cities, Paris doesn't really have a shopping 'centre': browsing is a fascinating way to discover hidden parts of the city. Many *quartiers* still specialise in a single product or art, and the myriad boutiques – still the heart and soul of Paris shopping – are often worth a visit in themselves.

Credit cards are accepted everywhere (Visa is the most common), but not travellers cheques. Many stores, in particular large department stores and 'duty-free' stores, will give foreign-passport holders discounts of 10% if asked; but bargaining is frowned upon, except at flea markets.

Hot Shop Spots

Paris' main shopping areas are:

Abbesses, 18e (4, D4) – vintage clothing, streetwear, fabrics, music

Marais, 3e (5, C8) – hip boutiques, books, music, homewares, quirky speciality stores

Opéra, 9e (3, C9) – major department stores, clothing, perfume, cosmetics

Place Vendôme, 1er (3, C8) – jewellery, luxury goods

Quartier Latin, 5e (5, D3) – books, stationery

rue de Paradis, 10e (3, A12) – glass, crystal, china, Limoges ware

rue de Rivoli & Les Halles, 1er & 2e (5, A6) – international brands, clothes, shoes, books, music, toys, perfume

St-Germain, 6e (5, C4) – designer clothes & accessories, shoes, antiques, speciality stores

St-Paul, 4e (3, G14) – antiques, paper goods, stationery

Sentier, 2e (3, C11) – wholesale garments, fabrics, jewellery

Triangle d'Or & rue du Faubourg St-Honoré, 8e & 1er (3, C3) – haute couture, jewellery, luxury goods, art galleries

Viaduc des Arts, 12e (2, G12) – boutiques, designers, galleries

Simon Bracken

DEPARTMENT STORES

Au Bon Marché (3, G7)
Paris' first department store, built by Gustave Eiffel, is less frenetic than its rivals across the river, and perhaps the most chic. Men's as well as women's fashions are well represented. The glorious grocery store, **La Grande Épicerie de Paris** (store No 2), has all your picnic needs.
✉ **24 rue de Sèvres, 7e**
☎ **01 44 39 80 00**
e www.lebonmarche.fr
Ⓜ **Sèvres Babylone**
🕐 **Mon-Wed & Fri 9.30am-7pm, Thurs 10am-9pm, Sat 9.30am-8pm; grocery store 8.30am-9pm**

BHV (5, C7)
Bazar de l'Hôtel de Ville is a straightforward department store, except that it has an enormous and chaotic hardware/DIY department in the *sous sol* (basement), with every type of tool, fixing and fitting you could ever need.
✉ **2-64 rue de Rivoli, 4e**
☎ **01 42 74 90 00**
e www.bhv.fr
Ⓜ **Hôtel de Ville**
🕐 **Mon-Sat 9.30am-7pm (Wed & Fri to 8.30pm)**

Forum des Halles
(5, A7) Not a department store, but the closest thing Paris has to an American-style shopping mall (albeit underground). The Halles has an enormous FNAC for books and music, Darty for electrical goods, many dozens of boutiques and food outlets and two multiplex cinemas.
✉ **rues Berger & Rambuteau, 1er**
☎ **01 44 76 96 56**
Ⓜ **Les Halles** 🕐 **Mon-Sat 10am-7.30pm**

The glorious Galeries

Galeries Lafayette
(3, B9) This vast store, with over 75,000 brand-name items, has everything under two roofs: fashion (Vivienne Westwood to Gap), shoes and accessories, perfume and cosmetics, lingerie, men's clothing, homewares, books and music – the lot. There's a fantastic view from the rooftop restaurants.
✉ **40 blvd Haussmann, 9e** ☎ **01 42 82 34 56**
e www.galeries lafayette.com Ⓜ **Auber, Chaussée d'Antin**
🕐 **Mon-Sat 9.30am-7pm (to 9pm Thurs)**

Le Printemps (3, B8)
Actually three separate stores – one each for women's and men's fashion and one for the home – Printemps offers a staggering display of perfume, cosmetics and accessories, as well as established and up-and-coming designer wear. There's a fashion show under the 7th floor cupola at 10am every Tues (and Fri Mar-Oct).
✉ **64 blvd Haussmann, 9e** ☎ **01 42 82 50 00**
e www.printemps.com
Ⓜ **Havre Caumartin**
🕐 **Mon-Sat 9.35am-7pm (to 10pm Thurs)**

La Samaritaine (5, A6)
It may not have the status of Galeries Lafayette or Printemps, but Samaritaine offers an excellent range across its three stores. There's a stunning (and free) view from the rooftop terrace of the main store, while the newly renovated Rivoli store is dedicated to men.
✉ **19 rue de la Monnaie, 1er** ☎ **01 40 41 20 20**
Ⓜ **Pont Neuf**
🕐 **Mon-Sat 9.30am-7pm (to 10pm Thurs)**

Opening Hours

Opening hours in Paris are notoriously anarchic, with each store setting its own hours according to some ancient black art. Most stores open at least 10am-7pm, five days a week, including Saturday; but they may open earlier, close later, close for lunch (usually 1-2.30pm) or for a full or half-day on Monday or Tuesday.

Many larger stores also have a *nocturne* – one late night a week (up to 9pm). Many smaller stores close completely in August. Only shops in some tourist areas (eg the Champs Élysées and the Marais) open on Sunday.

FASHION

Fashion is what Paris does best. In addition to the couturier addresses and the boutiques listed here, the large department stores have great ready-to-wear selections.

Abou Dhabi (5, D8)
Not what the name might imply – but a treasure trove of smart and affordable ready-to-wear pieces from young designers, including Paul & Joe and Tara Jarmon.
✉ **10 rue des Francs-Bourgeois, 3e** ☎ **01 42 77 96 98** Ⓜ **St-Paul**
🕐 **Sun-Mon 2-7pm, Tues-Sat 10.30am-7pm**

Absinthe (3, C9)
A lovely little boutique showcasing young French, Belgian and Spanish designers, such as Josep

Font and Julie Skarland.
✉ **74-76 rue Jean-Jacques Rousseau, 1er**
☎ **01 42 33 54 44**
Ⓜ **Le Halles**
🕐 **Mon-Fri 11am-7.30pm, Sat 11am-1pm & 2.30-7.30pm**

Antik Batik (5, E8)
Soft fabrics, soft colours – all the makings for the ethnic, hippy or gypsy look.
✉ **18 rue de Turenne, 3e**
☎ **01 44 78 02 00**
Ⓜ **Bastille, Chemin Vert**
🕐 **Tues-Sat 11am-7pm, Sun 2-7pm**

Didier Ludot (3, D9)
A fabulous store crammed with pre-loved couture creations from yesteryear, including original Chanel suits from the 1950s and Hermès bags and accessories – all sold for half the original price.
✉ **20-24 Galerie de Montpensier, 1er**
☎ **01 42 96 06 56**
Ⓜ **Palais Royal**
🕐 **Mon-Sat 11am-7pm**

L'Éclaireur (5, D7)
Part art space, part lounge, part deconstructionist fashion statement, this funky little boutique features the work of several young designers, as well as some handsome limited-edition jewellery.
✉ **3-ter rue des Rosiers, 4e** ☎ **01 48 87 10 22**
Ⓜ **St-Paul**
🕐 **Tues-Sat 11am-9pm**

Kiliwatch (3, D11)
Enormous barn filled with rack after rack of colourfully original street and clubwear, plus a startling range of quality second-hand clothes and accessories.
✉ **64 rue Tiquetonne, 2e**
☎ **01 42 21 17 37**
Ⓜ **Étienne Marcel**
🕐 **Mon 2-7pm, Tues-Sat 11am-7pm**

Madelios (3, C8)
One-stop shop for men, including a fine selection of classic and modern suits, shoes and casual wear, a hairdressing/beauty salon, cafe and exhibition space.
✉ **23 blvd de la**

A Cut Above

Top designer addresses include:
agnès b 6 rue du Jour, 1er (3, D11)
Barbara Bui 50 av Montaigne, 8e (3,C4)
Calvin Klein 45 av Montaigne, 8e (3, C4)
Chanel 31 rue Cambon, 1e (3, C8)
Christian Dior 30 av Montaigne, 8e (3, C4)
Dolce e Gabbana 2 av Montaigne, 8e (3, C4)
Emporio Armani 149 blvd St-Germain, 6e (5, A3)
Givenchy 8 av Georges V, 8e (3, C3)
Hermès 24 rue du Faubourg St-Honoré, 8e (3, C6)
Issey Miyake 3 Place des Vosges, 4e (5, E8)
Jean-Paul Gaultier 30 rue du Faubourg St-Antoine, 12e (2, F12)
Kenzo 3 Place des Victoires, 1er (3, D10)
Louis Vuitton 101 av des Champs Élysées, 8e (3, B4)
Paco Rabanne 7 rue du Cherche-Midi, 6e (3, G8)
Paul Smith 22 blvd raspail, 7e (3, G8)
Prada 10 av Montaigne, 8e (3, C4)
Sonia Rykiel 175 blvd St-Germain, 6e (3, F8)
Thierry Mugler 49 av Montaigne, 8e (3, C4)
Yohji Yamamoto 3 rue de Grenelle, 6e (3, G8)
Yves Saint Laurent 38 rue du Faubourg St-Honoré (3, C6)
Yves Saint Laurent Rive Gauche 6 Place St-Sulpice, 6e (5, A2)

Madeleine, 8e
☎ 01 53 45 00 00
Ⓜ Madeleine
🕐 10.30am-7pm

Le Mouton à Cinq Pattes (5, B3)

'The Sheep with Five Legs' specialises in heavily discounted designer clothing from last year's range. All items are new but most are *dégriffé* (their labels have been torn out). If you are lucky enough to know your Jean-Paul Gaultier from your Vivienne Westwood, you might just leg it with an absolute steal – many items being discounted by up to 70%.
✉ 8 rue St-Placide, 6e
☎ 01 45 48 20 49
Ⓜ Sèvres Babylone
🕐 Mon-Sat 10am-7pm

Réciproque (2, E4)

Réciproque has a comprehensive range of high-quality second-hand couture and designer clothing, shoes and accessories. Wares are available for

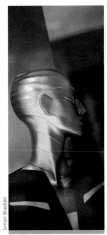

There are many ways to get ahead of the haute couture *crowd.*

both women and men and all are at around half the original price.
✉ 95 rue de la Pompe, 16e ☎ 01 47 04 30 28
Ⓜ Rue de la Pompe
🕐 Tues-Sat 11am-9pm

Spleen Shop (5, D7)

There are definitely no internal organs on sale at this shop with the visceral-sounding name. What you will find at Spleen is a stunningly showcased range of new *créateurs*, many from Italy and the UK, among them John Richmond, Lawrence Steele, Emilio Cavallini and Joerg Hartmann. There's also a hanging space for original fashion photography.
✉ 3bis rue des Rosiers, 4e ☎ 01 42 74 65 66
Ⓜ St-Paul
🕐 Sun-Mon 3-7pm, Tues-Sat 11am-7pm

Tati (4, D9)

With its war cry of *les plus*

bas prix (lowest prices) – and quality to match – Tati has been Paris' great working-class clothing store for 50 years. Don't be at all surprised to see trendy Parisians in search of street cred fighting for bargains in the oddments bins. There is also a branch in the 3e at 13 Place de la République.
✉ 4 blvd Barbès, 18e
☎ 01 55 29 50 00
e www.tati.fr
Ⓜ Barbès Rochechouart
🕐 Mon-Sat 10am-7.15pm

Victoire (3, D10)

Victoire offers stylish and classical label-browsing on the peaceful Place des Victoires for women, or at 15 rue du Vieux Colombier, 6e for men. There are a number of branches throughout Paris.
✉ 10-12 Place des Victoires, 2e ☎ 01 42 60 96 21 (women), 01 45 44 28 02 (men)
Ⓜ Bourse 🕐 Mon-sat 10.30am-7pm

Lacroix luxury

Lacey in Lacroix

ACCESSORIES

Camper (5, E8)
The Spanish name on everyone's feet – comfort, colour and casual wear are the watchwords.
✉ **9 rue des Francs-Bourgeois, 4e**
☎ **01 48 87 09 09**
Ⓜ **St-Paul, Bastille**
◷ **Mon-Sat 10.30am-7pm, Sun 2-7pm**

Cécile et Jeanne
(3, D8) Cécile and Jeanne are two young designers making a splash with their colourful and arty jewellery and accessories. They have several locations in the city. Also at 12 rue des Francs Bourgeois, 3e (3, F14); 49 av Daumesnil (Viaduc des Arts), 12e (2, G12).
✉ **215 rue St-Honoré, 1er** ☎ **01 42 61 68 68 (1er)** Ⓜ **Tuileries, St-Paul, Bastille**
◷ **Mon-Sat 11am-7pm**

Dazzling delights from two bright lights

Rob Flynn

Détaxe
If you're not a resident of the EU, you can get a TVA (sales tax) refund of up to 17%, provided you have spent more than €182 in any one store. You fill out a *détaxe* form in the store (you'll need your passport number), and then take the form and purchased goods to the customs desk at the point you leave the EU (allow at least 3hrs before flights). The refund is usually credited to your credit-card account or mailed by cheque within three months of you leaving the EU.

Colette (3, D8)
Japanese-inspired Colette is an ode to style over all else. Its selection and display of clothes, accessories and odds & ends is exquisite. Featured designers include Alexander McQueen, Marko Matysik and Lulu Guinness.
✉ **213 rue St-Honoré, 1er** ☎ **01 55 35 33 90**
Ⓜ **Tuileries** ◷ **Mon-Sat 10.30am-7.30pm**

Divine (2, H8)
An extraordinarily comprehensive range of new and pre-doffed headwear for both men and women, from straw boaters to Basque berets and velvet cloches.
✉ **39 rue Daguerre, 14e** ☎ **01 43 22 28 10**
Ⓜ **Denfert Rochereau**
◷ **Tues-Sat 10.30am-1pm & 3-7.30pm**

Il pour l'Homme
(3, D8) Housed in an old paint shop with 19th-century display counters and chests of drawers, 'It for the Man' has, well, everything a man could want or not need – from tie clips and cigar cutters to DIY tools and designer tweezers.
✉ **209 rue St-Honoré, 1er** ☎ **01 42 60 43 56**
Ⓜ **Tuileries** ◷ **Mon-Sat 10am-7pm**

Jamin Puech (3, A12)
Handbag as work of art? Assert your individuality with a completely original *sac* in an innovative range of fabrics and designs.
✉ **61 rue d'Hauteville, 10e** ☎ **01 40 22 08 32**
Ⓜ **Poissonière**
◷ **Mon & Sat 11am-7pm, Tues-Fri 10am-7pm**

BEAUTY & PERFUME

Guerlain (3, B4)
Guerlain is Paris' most famous perfumerie, and its shop, dating from 1912, is one of the most beautiful in the city. With its shimmering mirror and marble decor it's a reminder of the former glory of the Champs Élysées. Many Guerlain fragrances are available only through Guerlain boutiques. ⊠ **68 av des Champs Élysées, 8e** ☎ **01 45 62 52 57** Ⓜ **Franklin D Roosevelt** ⏰ **10am-8pm**

l'Artisan Parfumeur
(5, C7) Warm and sensual fragrances for the body and the home, including *mûre et musc* (blackberry & musk), fig, tea and rose. ⊠ **32 rue du Bourg Tibourg, 4e** ☎ **01 48 04 55 66** Ⓜ **St-Paul** ⏰ **Mon-Sat 10.30am-7pm**

Beauty By Et Vous
(3, C7) Ultra *tendance* (trendy) beauty/fashion concept store – think video screens and mannequins hung from the ceiling – for cutting edge cosmetics,

Coco's classic

aromatherapy, accessories and clothes. ⊠ **25 rue Royale, 8e** ☎ **01 47 42 31 00** Ⓜ **Madeleine** ⏰ **Mon-Sat 10.30am-7.30pm**

Séphora (3, B4)
Séphora's flagship megastore features over 12,000 fragrances and cosmetics, most of which are available for sampling with no pressure to buy. Branches throughout Paris. ⊠ **70 av des Champs Élysées, 8e**

☎ **01 53 93 22 50** Ⓜ **Franklin D Roosevelt** ⏰ **Mon-Sat 10am-1am, Sun noon-1am**

Shiseido (3, D10)
This exquisite salon in the arcades of the Palais Royal is the showcase for the olfactory genius of Serge Lutens, and well worth a visit just for a sniff – or for a custom-designed scent. ⊠ **142 Galerie de Valois, 1er** ☎ **01 49 27 09 09** Ⓜ **Louvre, Palais Royal** ⏰ **Mon-Sat 9am-7pm**

Shu Uemura (5, A3)
Colour your world with the palettes of this cult Japanese make-up magician who offers over 100 shades of lippie, blusher and eyeshadow. Have half your face made up by the knowledgeable beauticians, and do the other half yourself under their watchful eye (bookings in advance). ⊠ **176 blvd St-Germain, 6e** ☎ **01 45 48 02 55** Ⓜ **St-Germain des Prés** ⏰ **Mon 11am-7pm, Tues-Wed 10am-7pm, Thurs-Sat 10am-8pm**

ART & ANTIQUES

Paris' high-quality antique dealers congregate in the rue du Faubourg St-Honoré (8e) and the Carré Rive Gauche (just to the east of the Musée d'Orsay, 7e) and the Village St-Paul (4e).

Art galleries cluster around av Matignon (8e), Beaubourg (3e), St-Germain (6e), Bastille (11e/12e) and rue Louise Weiss (13e). Exhibitions are listed in *Pariscope* and *L'Officiel des Spectacles*. Many galleries close in August.

Drouot-Richelieu
(3, B10) Paris' best known auction house has been selling fine lots for nearly 150 years. Bidding is in (fast) French and a 10-15% house commission is

charged on top of the purchase price. Payment in cash or by French bank cheque only. Auction details are in the *Gazette de l'Hôtel Drouot* at newsstands. ⊠ **9 rue Drouot, 9e**

☎ **01 48 00 20 20** ℮ **www.gazette-drouot.com** Ⓜ **Richelieu Drouot** ⏰ **sales 2-6pm; viewing 11am-6pm day prior & 11am-noon sale day**

Galerie Adrian Maeght (3, F8)

One of the best known galleries in Paris – where the work of Braque, Giacometti, Del Rey and Miró once hung – still displays an impressive array of modern works; there's also a fine art bookstore.

✉ 42 rue du Bac, 7e
☎ 01 45 48 45 15
Ⓜ Rue du Bac ⏱ Mon 10am-6pm, Tues-Sat 9am-6.30pm

Galerie Durand-Dessert (2, F12)

Probably the strongest of the new-wave Bastille-quarter galleries, it features the work of many exciting artists including Yan Pei Ming and Gérard Garouste, and top photographers William Wegman, Patrick Tosani and Balthasar Burkhard.

✉ 28 rue de Lappe, 11e
☎ 01 48 06 92 23
Ⓜ Bastille
⏱ Tues-Sat 11am-7pm

Galerie Jennifer Flay (2, H12)

What's a Kiwi doing flogging conceptual art in Paris? A very fine job, according to the cognoscenti. Jennifer Flay offers a good intro to (and explanation of) the *ScèneEst* scene.

✉ 20 rue Louise Weiss, 13e ☎ 01 44 06 73 60
Ⓜ Chevaleret
⏱ Tues-Sat 11am-7pm

Le Louvre des Antiquaires (3, E10)

Some 250 elegant antique shops cluster on three floors of this impressive building on the eastern side of Place du Palais Royal. Each is filled with original (and expensive) furniture, clocks, *objets d'art*, classical antiquities and (in the basement) jewellery.

✉ 2 Place du Palais Royal, 1er ☎ 01 42 97 27 00 🌐 www.louvre -antiquaires.com
Ⓜ Palais Royal
⏱ Tues-Sun 11am-7pm

Time Passages

Paris' *passages* or *galeries* are 19th-century shopping arcades, many sublimely preserved and well worth a detour.

Galerie Véro Dodat (3, D10; 19 rue Jean-Jacques Rousseau to 2 rue du Bouloi, 1er) opened in 1826 and specialises in antiques, *objets d'art*, and fashion accessories. In the **Passage du Grand Cerf** (3, D12; 145 rue St-Denis to 10 rue Dussoubs, 2e) you'll find modern jewellery and lighting designers; while the gorgeous **Galerie Vivienne** (3, D10; 6 rue Vivienne to 4 rue des Petits Champs, 2e) has a fashion bent.

BOOKS

Abbey Bookshop

(5, C4) Not far from Place St-Michel, this mellow place is known for having free tea and coffee, a supply of Canadian newspapers and a good selection of new and used works of fiction – plus readings of prose and poetry once a week, usually on Wednesday night.

✉ 29 rue de la Parcheminerie, 5e
☎ 01 46 33 16 24
Ⓜ Cluny-La Sorbonne
⏱ Mon-Sat 10am-7pm

Album (5, C4)

This shop specialises in adult *bandes dessinées* (comic books), which have an enormous following in France. Album has everything from *Tintin,* to erotic and rare comics, to French editions of the latest Japanese *manga*.

✉ 8 rue Dante, 5e
☎ 01 43 25 85 19
Ⓜ Maubert-Mutualité
⏱ Mon-Sat 10am-8pm

Brentano's (3, C9)

Midway between the Louvre and Opéra Garnier, this is a good spot for tracking down books from the USA, including fiction, business titles and magazines. There's also a good range of kids' books.

✉ 37 av de l'Opéra, 2e
☎ 01 42 61 52 50

Ⓜ Opéra ⏱ Mon-Sat 10am-7.30pm

Institut Géographique National (3, B4)

A cartographer's delight – atlases, globes, walking maps, wine district maps, compasses, satellite images, historic maps and guidebooks to France and the rest of the world.

✉ 107 rue la Boétie, 8e ☎ 01 43 98 85 00
🌐 www.ign.fr
Ⓜ Franklin D Roosevelt
⏱ Mon-Fri 9.30am-7pm

Librarie Gourmande

(5, C4) Not only do the French love to talk about

food, they love to write about it as well, and Geneviève Baudon's tasteful bookshop is *the* place to discover the secrets of French food, wine and the culinary arts.

✉ 4 rue Dante, 5e
☎ 01 43 54 37 27
Ⓜ Maubert Mutualité
◷ Mon-Sat 10am-7pm

Les Mots à la Bouche (5, C7) Paris' premier gay bookshop specialises in books written by homosexuals or with gay or lesbian themes, and periodicals, including some in English. Most of the back wall is dedicated to English-language books, including lots of novels. Videos and CDs are also on sale.

✉ 6 rue Ste-Croix de la Bretonnerie, 4e
☎ 01 42 78 88 30
Ⓜ Hôtel de Ville
◷ Mon-Sat 11am-10pm, Sun 2-8pm

Shakespeare & Company (5, C5) Paris' most famous English-language bookshop has a varied and unpredictable collection of new and used books in English and other languages. Poetry readings are held on most Mondays at 8pm. The shop is named after Sylvia Beach's bookshop – famous for publishing James Joyce's *Ulysses* in 1922 – which was closed by the Nazis in 1941.

✉ 37 rue de la Bûcherie, 5e ☎ 01 43 26 96 50 Ⓜ St-Michel
◷ noon-midnight

Village Voice (5, A3) A friendly, helpful shop with an excellent selection of contemporary North American fiction and European literature in translation. It often sponsors readings, often on Thursday at around 7pm.

✉ 6 rue Princesse, 6e
☎ 01 46 33 36 47
Ⓜ Mabillon
◷ Mon 2-8pm, Tues-Sat 10am-8pm, Sun 2-7pm (except Aug)

WH Smith (3, D7) This branch of the English chain, one block east of Place de la Concorde, offers a large selection of English-language titles and magazines. Brace yourself for the imported prices.

✉ 248 rue de Rivoli, 1er
☎ 01 44 77 88 99
Ⓜ Concorde
◷ Mon-Sat 9am-7.30pm, Sun 1-7.30pm

Chief cataloguer

Ulysse (5, E6) For 20 years Catherine Demain has been fuelling the wanderlust of Parisian travellers in this delightful store full of travel guides, maps, back issues of *National Geographic* and sage advice.

✉ 26 rue St-Louis en l'Île, 4e ☎ 01 43 25 17 35
e www.ulysse.fr
Ⓜ Pont Marie
◷ Tues-Sat 2-8pm

Where there's a Will, there's a load of quality literature.

MUSIC

La Chaumière (3, H10)
Comprehensive catalogue of classical music and very knowledgeable staff.
✉ 5 rue de Vaugirard, 6e ☎ 01 43 54 07 25
🕐 Mon-Sat 11am-8pm, Sun 2-8pm

Crocodisc (5, D4)
Good selection of new and used African, Oriental, Caribbean and soul as well as pop and rock. For jazz and blues try **Crocojazz**, just around the corner (64 rue de la Montagne Ste-Geneviève).
✉ 40-42 rue des Écoles, 5e ☎ 01 43 54 47 95
Ⓜ Maubert-Mutualité
🕐 Tues-Sat 11am-7pm

FNAC Musique (3, G15) FNAC music is France's largest book and music chain. Its flagship music store at Bastille has a huge variety of local and international music. The branch at Les Halles (5, A7) is also well stocked. Concert booking desk.
✉ 4 Place de la Bastille, 12e ☎ 01 49 54 30 00
🄴 www.fnac.fr
Ⓜ Bastille 🕐 Mon-Sat 10am-8pm (to 10pm Wed)

Virgin Megastore (3, B4) This French-owned version of the humungous British music and bookstore multinational chain has the largest music collection in Paris, as well as English-language books and magazines and a decent cafe/restaurant.
✉ 52-60 av des Champs-Élysées, 8e ☎ 01 49 53 50 00
🄴 www.virgin.fr
Ⓜ Franklin D Roosevelt, George V
🕐 Mon-Sat 10am-midnight, Sun noon-midnight

HOMEWARES & DESIGN

Autour du Monde (5, D8) There's a little bit of everything in this eminently browseable homewares store, with Oriental, European and international influences.
✉ 8 rue des Francs-Bourgeois, 4e ☎ 01 42 77 16 18
Ⓜ Hôtel de Ville 🕐 Mon-Sat 10.30am-7pm, Sun 1-7pm

Bains Plus (5, D8)
Bathroom suppliers to the hip and freshly washed, including luxurious robes and gowns, soaps and oils, shaving brushes, mirrors...
✉ 51 rue des Francs Bourgeois, 3e ☎ 01 48 87 83 07
Ⓜ Hôtel de Ville 🕐 Tues-Sat 11am-7pm, Sun 2.30-7pm

E Dehillerin (3, D11)
This shop (founded in 1820) carries the most incredible selection of professional-quality cookware – you're sure to find something even the best equipped kitchen is lacking.
✉ 18-20 rue Coquillière, 1er ☎ 01 42 36 53 13
Ⓜ Les Halles 🕐 Mon-Sat 8am-6pm (closed Mon 12.30-2pm)

Les Milles Feuilles (5, C8) Wonderfully disorganised little shop full of romantic gift ideas (for yourself, of course): baskets, candles, flowers, vases and what-nots.
✉ 2 rue Rambuteau, 3e ☎ 01 42 78 32 93
Ⓜ Rambuteau 🕐 10am-8pm (Mon from 11am)

A Simon (3, D11)
Supplier of kitchenware with more saucepans and mixing bowls than you thought imaginable.
✉ 36 rue Étienne Marcel, 2e ☎ 01 42 33 71 65 Ⓜ Étienne Marcel 🕐 Mon-Sat 8.30am-6.30pm

Home is where the art is.

Rob Flynn

FOR CHILDREN

Au Nain Bleu (3, C8)

Just what you'd imagine Paris' oldest toy shop (opened 1836) would look like. Good selection of traditional and modern toys.
⊠ **406-10 rue St-Honoré, 8e** ☎ **01 42 60 39 01** ⓜ **Madeleine** ◷ Mon-Sat 9.45am-6.30pm

Chantelivre (3, G8)

Chantelivre is a bookshop for and about children, with a reasonably good English-language selection. The range includes picture books, novels and videos as well as child psychology and parenting tomes. There's also a play area for nonbrowsing anklebiters.
⊠ **13 rue de Sèvres, 6e** ☎ **01 45 48 87 90** ⓜ **Sèvres Babylone** ◷ Mon-Sat 10am-7pm (Mon from 1pm)

Le Ciel est à Tout le Monde (5, D2)

If it flies – or looks like it might – you're bound to find it here: kites, boomerangs and frisbees abound. And there's an extraordinary range of toys and dolls (including Babar and Petit Prince ranges) and a bunch of other fun stuff.
⊠ **10 rue Gay Lussac, 5e** ☎ **01 46 33 21 50** ⓡ **RER Luxembourg** ◷ Mon-Sat 10am-7pm

Du Pareil au Même

(2, F12) The dozen or so branches of this chain offer colourful, fun and durable no-nonsense children's clothing at very reasonable prices.
⊠ **122 rue du Faubourg St-Antoine, 12e** ☎ **01 43 44 47 66** ⓜ **Ledru Rollin** ◷ Mon-Sat 10am-7pm

FNAC Junior (3, J8)

This kid-oriented branch of the massive FNAC retail chain does everything right with its excellent selection of books, videos, CD-ROMs and educational toys – including (shock horror!) letting kids actually play with them. There are organised activities (usually on Wednesday and Saturday), including multimedia play stations, storytelling and puppet shows.
⊠ **19 rue Vavin, 6e** ☎ **01 56 24 03 46** ⓜ **Vavin** ◷ Mon-Sat 10am-7.30pm

Pom d'Api (3, D11)

Fun colourful and strong shoes for young feet to size 40. There's also a range of kids' chairs in the shape of animals.
⊠ **13 rue du Jour, 1er** ☎ **01 42 36 08 87** ⓜ **Les Halles** ◷ Mon-Sat 10am-7pm

Si Tu Veux (3, D10)

Imaginative and creative activities for kids, most sold in kit form, plus costumes and traditional toys.
⊠ **68 Galerie Vivienne, 2e** ☎ **01 42 60 59 97** ⓜ **Bourse** ◷ Mon-Sat 10.30am-7pm

Late-Night Buys

Paris is definately not a 24hr city, and shops often close just minutes before you run out of something really essential – like chocolate. Here's a few addresses to try when you're desperate for something essential in the wee hours:

- **Boulangerie de l'Ancienne Comédie** (5, B3) 10 rue de l'Ancienne Comédie, 6e ☎ 01 43 26 89 72 ⓜ Odéon ◷ 24hrs – bread & pastries, snacks & sandwiches

- **Drugstore Publicis** (3, B3) 131 av des Champs Élysées, 8e ☎ 01 44 43 79 00 ⓜ Charles de Gaulle-Étoile ◷ 9am-2am – newspapers, books, cigarettes and bits & pieces.

- **News Kiosque** (3, B3) Place Charles de Gaulle, 8e ⓜ Charles de Gaulle-Étoile ◷ 24hrs – newspapers & magazines

- **Monoprix** (3, B4) 109 rue de la Boétie, 8e ☎ 01 53 77 65 65 ⓜ Franklin D Roosevelt ◷ Mon-Sun 9am-midnight (Sun from 10am) – all supermarket needs

- **Shell Garage** (3, F8) 6 blvd Raspail, 7e ☎ 01 45 48 43 12 ⓜ Rue du Bac ◷ 24hrs – petrol, drinks, sweets & snacks

FOOD & DRINK

À l'Olivier (5, D7)
The place in Paris for oil – from olive to walnut – with a good selection of vinegars, olives and mustards as well.
✉ **23 rue de Rivoli, 4e**
☎ **01 48 04 86 59**
Ⓜ **St-Paul** ☼ **Tues-Sat 9.30am-7pm**

Les Caves Augé (3, A6)
If Marcel Proust was any judge of wine shops, then go no further than Paris' oldest – now under the stewardship of passionate and knowledgeable *sommelier* Marc Sibard.
✉ **116 blvd Haussmann, 8e** ☎ **01 45 22 16 97**
Ⓜ **St-Augustin**
☼ **Mon-Sat 9am-7.30pm (Mon from 1pm)**

Fauchon (3, B8)
The most famous food store in Paris: six departments sell the most incredibly mouthwatering (and expensive) delicacies, from *foie gras* to *confitures*. The fruits – the most perfect you've ever seen – include exotic items from South-East Asia (mangosteens, rambutans etc). Fauchon also has several eat-in options.
✉ **26-30 Place de la Madeleine, 8e**
☎ **01 47 42 60 11**
Ⓜ **Madeleine**
☼ **Mon-Sat 8.30am-7pm**

La Grande Épicerie de Paris (3, H7)
Get all your picnic supplies at this wonderful Left Bank gourmet delicatessen and supermarket. Pack it up and pack yourself off to a park or public square.
✉ **Store 2 Au Bon Marché, 38 rue de Sèvres, 7e** ☎ **01 44 39 81 00**
Ⓜ **Sèvres Babylone**
☼ **Mon-Sat 8.30am-9pm**

Hédiard (3, B7)
This famous luxury food shop consists of two adjacent sections selling prepared dishes, tea, coffee, jams, wine, pastries, fruit and vegetables etc. Branches throughout Paris.
✉ **21 Place de la Madeleine, 8e**
☎ **01 43 12 88 88**
Ⓜ **Madeleine**
☼ **Mon-Sat 9am-9.30pm, Sun 9am-9pm**

Maison de la Truffe
(3, B7) If you've always wanted to snuffle fine truffles – French black from late October to March, Italian white mid-October to December (over €300 per 100g) – here's your chance. There's also a small sit-down area (open from noon to closing) where you can sample dishes made with the prized fungus.
✉ **19-21 Place de la Madeleine, 8e**
☎ **01 42 65 53 22**
Ⓜ **Madeleine**
☼ **Mon-Sat 9am-9pm (to 8pm Mon)**

Rob Flynn

Tea for two or tea for tout le monde?

French dairy products are la crème de la crème.

Mariage Frères (5, C7)

Paris' premier tea shop (founded in 1854) has around 500 varieties from 32 countries; the most expensive is a variety of Japanese *thé vert* (green tea) which costs about €7.50 for 100g. In summer you can cool off in the 19th-century *salon de thé* (tearoom) with a choice of five kinds of tea-flavoured ice cream. There are branches at 13 rue des Grands Augustins (6e) and 260 rue du Faubourg-St-Honoré (8e).

✉ **30-32 rue du Bourg Tibourg, 4e**
☎ **01 42 72 28 11**
Ⓜ **Hôtel de Ville**
◷ **10.30am-7.30pm, tearoom 12-7pm**

Au Levain du Marais

(5, E8) The patient punters waiting outside this Marais *boulangerie* know exactly where to find the best baguettes in the quarter, as well as wonderful speciality breads and delicious pastries with seasonal fruits.

✉ **32 rue de Turenne, 3e**
☎ **01 42 78 07 31**
Ⓜ **St-Paul**
◷ **Mon-Sat 7am-8pm**

Cacao et Chocolat

(5, A3) Here's a contemporary exotic take on choccy, showcasing the bean in all its seductive guises, both solid and liquid. The added citrus notes, spices and even chilli are guaranteed to tease you back for more.

✉ **29 rue du Buci, 6e**
☎ **01 46 33 77 63**
Ⓜ **Mabillon** ◷ **Tues-Sat 10am-7.30pm**

Dalloyau (3, B5)

The five branches around Paris (now at place de la Bastille) of this venerable *pâtisserie* (established in 1802) fuel the desire for some of Paris' best croissants, *pain aux raisins*, chocolates and other sinful goodies.

✉ **101 rue du Faubourg St-Honoré, 8e** ☎ **01 42 99 90 00** Ⓜ **St-Philippe du Roule** ◷ **8.30am-9pm**

Jadis et Gourmande

(3, K9) One of four branches that sell chocolate, chocolate and more chocolate in every conceivable shape and size, plus cocoa from around the world and novelty items like chocolate postcards.

✉ **88 blvd de Port Royal, 5e** ☎ **01 43 26 17 75**
Ⓜ **Port Royal**
◷ **Mon 1-7pm, Tues-Wed 9.30am-7pm, Thurs-Sat 9.30am-7.30pm**

Poilàne (3, G8)

Truly a legend in his own lunchtime, Lionel Poilàne bakes perfect wholegrain bread using traditional sourdough leavening and sea salt. Every loaf is an original, but they're all delicious. Pain Poilàne is also available from selected outlets throughout Paris.

✉ **8 rue du Cherche-Midi, 6e**
☎ **01 45 48 42 59**
Ⓜ **St-Sulpice, Sèvres Babylone** ◷ **Mon-Sat 7.15am-8.15pm**

Divine Hédiard

FLEA MARKETS

Paris' *marchés aux puces* (flea markets), easily accessible by metro, can be great fun if you're in the mood to browse for unexpected treasures among the *brocante* (second-hand goods) and bric-a-brac on display. Some new goods are also available, and a bit of bargaining is expected.

Marché aux Puces de Montreuil (2, F15)
Established in the 19th century, this market is in the south-eastern corner of the 20e, between the Porte de Montreuil metro stop and the ring road. It is known for having good-quality second-hand clothes and designer seconds. The 500 stalls also sell engravings, jewellery, linen, crockery, old furniture and appliances.
✉ av de la Porte de Montreuil, 20e
Ⓜ Porte de Montreuil
🕐 Sat-Mon 7am-7pm

Marché aux Puces de St-Ouen (2, A9)
This vast flea market, founded in the late 19th century and said to be Europe's largest, is at the northern edge of the 18e. The 2000-odd stalls are grouped into nine *marchés* (market areas), each with its own specialities (antiques, cheap clothing etc). While shopping, watch out for pickpockets.
✉ rue des Rosiers, av Michelet, rue Voltaire, rue Paul Bert & rue Jean-Henri Fabre, 18e
Ⓜ Porte de Clignancourt
🕐 Sat-Mon 7.30am-7pm

Marché aux Puces de la Porte de Vanves (2, J7) This market in the far southwestern corner of the 14e is known for its fine selection of junk: av Georges Lafenestre looks like a giant car-boot sale, with lots of 'curios' which aren't quite old (or classy) enough to qualify as antiques, while av Marc Sangnier is lined with stalls selling new clothes, shoes, handbags and household items.
✉ av Georges Lafenestre & av Marc Sangnier, 14e
Ⓜ Porte de Vanves
🕐 Sat-Sun 7am-6pm

Marché d'Aligre (2, G12) Small but more central than Paris' other three flea markets, this market is one of the best places in Paris to rummage through cardboard boxes filled with old clothes and one-of-a-kind accessories worn decades ago by fashionable (and not-so-fashionable) Parisians.
✉ Place d'Aligre, 12e
Ⓜ Ledru Rollin
🕐 Tues-Sun early-1pm

I know there's a Braque in there somewhere! Try your luck at a roadside brocante.

Rob Flynn

SPECIALIST STORES

One of the joys of shopping in Paris is the unexpected boutiques specialising in arcane products or arts.

Anna Joliet (3, D10)
This wonderful little shop specialises in music boxes, both new and old, for romantics and children alike. Just open the door and see if you aren't tempted in.
✉ **9 rue de Beaujolais, 1er** ☎ **01 42 96 55 13**
Ⓜ **Pyramides**
◷ Mon-Sat 10am-7pm

Au Vieux Campeur
(5, C4) This camping chain has 17 shops in the Quartier Latin, just east of rue St-Jacques between blvd St-Germain and rue des Écoles. Each specialises in equipment for a specific kind of outdoor activity: hiking, mountaineering, cycling, skiing, snowboarding, scuba diving etc.
✉ **48 rue des Écoles, 5e** ☎ **01 43 29 12 32**
Ⓜ **Cluny-La Sorbonne**
◷ Tues-Fri 11am-7.30pm (to 9pm Wed), Sat 9.30am-7.30pm

EOL' Modelisme
(5, D4) This shop sells expensive toys for big boys and girls, including every sort of model imaginable – from radio-controlled aircraft to huge wooden yachts. The main shop, right by the metro entrance, has an amazing collection of tiny cars.
✉ **55, 62 & 70 blvd St-Germain, 5e**
☎ **01 43 54 01 43**
Ⓜ **Maubert Mutualité**
◷ Mon-Fri 9am-8pm

Galerie Inard (3, G8)
This gallery sells stunning

Aubusson tapestries from the postwar period and imaginative, contemporary glass. You won't get much change from €50,000 for a medium-sized tapestry by a well-known artist.
✉ **179 blvd St-Germain, 6e** ☎ **01 40 20 40 34**
Ⓜ **St-Germain des Prés**
◷ Tues-Sat 10am-12.30pm & 2-7pm

Madeleine Gély (3, F8)
If you're in the market for a bespoke cane or umbrella, this shop (founded in 1834) will supply.
✉ **218 blvd St-Germain, 7e** ☎ **01 42 22 63 35**
Ⓜ **St-Germain des Prés**
◷ Tues-Sat 10am-7pm

Mélodies Graphiques
(5, D6) This shop carries all sorts of items made from exquisite Florentine *papier à cuve* (paper hand-decorated with marbled designs). It is nestled in among several other fine stationery shops along the same street.
✉ **10 rue du Pont Louis-Philippe, 4e**
☎ **01 42 74 57 68**
Ⓜ **Pont Marie**
◷ 11am-7pm (Sun-Mon from 2pm)

Odimex Paris
(5, B3) Just the place to stock up on teapots. Pot yourself a little one, a big one, a sophisticated one, a comic one or a very expensive one.
✉ **17 rue de l'Odéon, 6e** ☎ **1 46 33 98 96**
Ⓜ **Odéon** ◷ Mon-Sat 10am-1pm & 2pm-7pm

Robin des Bois (5, D7)
A shop strictly for environmentalists, this place sells everything and anything made from recycled things – from jewellery to stationery. There's something here to make every Green green with envy.
✉ **15 rue Fernand Duval, 4e**
☎ **01 48 04 09 36**
Ⓜ **St-Paul** ◷ Mon-Sat 10.30am-7.30pm, Sun 2-7.30pm

No need to take back tack.

Sennelier (3, F9)
If your visit to the Musée d'Orsay left you inspired, drop in at Sennelier to find the source of all those vibrant colours. This artists' colour merchant has been in business for well over a century, and still makes paints using rare pigments, as well as supplying other artists' materials.
✉ **3 Quai Voltaire, 7e**
☎ **01 42 60 72 15**
Ⓜ **St-Germain des Prés**
◷ Tues-Sat 9.30am-12.30pm & 2-6pm

places to eat

Food and eating are consuming passions for Parisians. An amazing amount of time is spent thinking and talking about food, with seemingly endless discussions about the merits of this particular restaurant or that particular dish. Lonely Planet's *Out to Eat – Paris* reviews hundreds of Paris' best restaurants, cafes and bars.

Cuisine

While many people think of a single 'French cuisine', the truth is that there are many – each based on the produce and gastronomy of the individual regions of the country. Fortunately, in Paris, you can sample them all. You can also feast on an exceptional variety of ethnic food, brought to Paris by successive waves of immigrants from France's former colonies and protectorates in Africa, Indochina, the Middle East, India, the Caribbean and the South Pacific. The French *petit déjeuner* (breakfast) often consists of nothing more than a strong black *café*, though a croissant, a light bread roll with jam, or a boiled egg might be added. For many people, lunch is still the main meal of the day. Dinner usually begins around 8.30pm.

Simon Bracken

L'addition S'il Vous Plaît

The price ranges used in this chapter indicate the average cost of a three-course meal for one person ordered à la carte (excluding alcohol).

$	under €20
$$	€20-30
$$$	€30-50
$$$$	over €50

Where to Eat

The quintessential Parisian place to eat is the **bistro**, which is usually a small neighbourhood restaurant open just for lunch (noon-2pm) and dinner (7.30-10.30pm), and offering a variety of meals à la carte or cheaper set-price *menus* (see p. 80). Bistros often specialise in the food of a particular region. **Brasseries** have their roots in Alsatian beer halls. They are often large places serving meals at all times of the day, often traditional fare such as *choucroute* (sauerkraut), oysters, and steak and *frites* (chips).

The **cafe** is an important focal point for social life, and sitting in one to read, write, talk with friends or merely watch the world go by is an integral part of many Parisians' day-to-day existence. Only basic food (sandwiches, salads, simple meals) is available in most cafes.

Tipping & Taxes

By law, all cafes, bars and restaurants include a 15% service charge *(service compris)* in your bill, making it unnecessary to tip; but by all means leave a little extra on the table for exceptional service.

Many restaurants are closed Sunday and Monday; reservations are recommended for dinner, especially later in the week. Many restaurants close for the entire month of August.

BASTILLE & FAUBOURG ST-ANTOINE

The area around Bastille is chock-a-block with restaurants. Narrow, scruffy rue de Lappe (2, F12) may not look like much during the day, but it's one of the trendiest cafe and nightlife streets in Paris, attracting a young, alternative crowd. Many of the places speak with a Spanish accent – Tex-Mex, tapas and Cuban food can all be found here. Things really start to pick up late at night.

Bali Bar (3, G15) $$$
Thai
Nothing to do with Indonesia (and not a bar) this former hairdressing school is one of the best new Thai restaurants in town, presided over by talented young chef Oth Sombath. The decor is colonial trading post and the food is carefully prepared and very tasty.
✉ 9 rue Saint-Sabin, 11e
☎ 01 47 00 25 47
Ⓜ Bastille ◷ Mon-Sat 7pm-2am Ⓥ

Le Bistrot du Dôme (3, G15) $$$
Seafood
This inviting restaurant specialises in superbly prepared seafood dishes. From the flavoursome fish soups to impeccable fish mains (accompanied by a perfectly chosen wine list) and delicious desserts, there's rarely a false note. Bookings essential.
✉ 2 rue de la Bastille, 4e ☎ 01 48 04 88 44
Ⓜ Bastille
◷ 12.30-2.30pm, 7.30-11.30pm

Brasserie Bofinger (3, G15) $$$
French
This is reputedly the oldest brasserie in Paris (founded in 1864), with original Art Deco brass, glass and mirrors, and it's still, deservedly, one of the most popular. Specialities include oysters, *choucroute* and seafood

---

Business & Bouffe
If your local Parisian partners are bereft of ideas (not!) you could suggest **L'Absinthe** (p. 76) in the financial district, **Joe Allen** (p. 76) for innovative American fare, **Le Bistrot du Dôme** (at left) and L'Enoteca near Bastille, or **Jaques Cagna** (p. 81) in the publishing heartland of the 6e. For a more relaxed meeting, suggest **Café Beaubourg** (p. 77) on the right bank or **Les Deux Magots** (p. 81) on the left.

---

dishes, and the *menu* includes a half-bottle of wine. Bookings advisable for dinner and Sun lunch. *Menu* €19/28.
✉ 5-7 rue de la Bastille, 4e ☎ 01 42 72 87 82
Ⓜ Bastille ◷ Mon-Fri noon-3pm & 6.30pm-1am; Sat-Sun noon-1am

L'Ébauchoir (2, G12) $$
French
Warm colours, small wooden tables, regular customers and smiling young staff are the first impressions of this convivial little neighbourhood bistro. The carefully prepared food is typical bistro fare – with a twist of originality: snails or fennel with lemon for starters, followed by veal liver with honey and coriander. Bookings advisable for dinner. Lunch *menu* €11.
✉ 45 rue de Cîteaux, 12e ☎ 01 43 42 49 31
Ⓜ Faidherbe Chaligny ◷ Tues-Sat noon-2.30pm & 8-11pm

L'Écailler du Bistrot (2, F13) $$
Seafood
This friendly little place might be a little off the beaten track, but it's worth searching out for its excellent range of fresh seafood, including a wide selection of oysters, grey shrimp, spider crabs, salmon (fresh *rillettes* or smoked *maison*), salt cod and other delicacies of the deep. Bookings advisable. Lunch *menu* €13.
✉ 22 rue Paul-Bert, 11e ☎ 01 43 72 76 77
Ⓜ Faidherbe Chaligny ◷ Tues-Sat noon-2.30pm, Mon-Sat 7.30-11.30pm

Lire entre les Vignes (3, F15) $$
Modern French
Hidden away in a nondescript Bastille street, 'Read Between the Vines' is an oasis of conviviality, reminiscent of a comfortable and spacious country kitchen, and a great spot to

dine with friends. The food is fresh, imaginative and tasty – prepared before your eyes in the corner kitchen. Bookings advisable. Lunch *menu* €13.

✉ **38 rue Sedaine, 11e**
☎ **01 43 55 69 49**
Ⓜ **Bréguet Sabin**

Meal Freebies

Bread (normally a sliced baguette) is provided free of charge with meals. Ask for more if you finish it or it's stale. You will normally need to ask for water (*une carafe d'eau*), which is also free of charge.

Simon Bracken

🕐 **Mon-Fri noon-2.30pm & 7.30-10.30pm, Sat 7.30-11pm**

Le Square Trousseau
(2, F12) $$
French

This vintage bistro, with its etched glass and polished wood panelling, is comfortable rather than trendy and attracts a mixed clientele, including some brand-name fashion icons. The carefully prepared food is of high quality, but most people come to enjoy the lovely terrace overlooking the eponymous square. Bookings advisable. *Menu* €16/20.

✉ **1 rue Antoine Vollon, 12e** ☎ **01 43 43 06 00**
Ⓜ **Ledru Rollin**
🕐 **11.30am-2pm & 7-10.30pm**

Suds (2, F12) $$
International

No, not a trendy laundrette but a very *branché* bar/restaurant with a name that means 'Souths', and

with jazz or Latin music in the basement. The cuisine here is anything and everything from the south – from Mexican and Peruvian to Portuguese and North African. Bookings required. Lunch *menu* €11.

✉ **55 rue de Charonne, 11e** ☎ **01 43 14 06 36**
Ⓜ **Ledru Rollin, Bastille**
🕐 **Tues-Fri noon-2pm, Tues-Sun 8pm-2am**

Swann & Vincent
(2, F12) $$
Italian

This open, light and friendly place offers great Italian food: tasty home-style breads, antipasto, a choice of pasta or meat mains, tiramisù and Italian wines. Bookings advisable. Weekday lunch *menu* €13.

✉ **7 rue St-Nicolas, 12e**
☎ **01 43 43 49 40**
Ⓜ **Ledru Rollin**
🕐 **lunch noon-2.45pm; dinner Sun-Wed 7.30-11.45pm &, Thurs-Sat 7.30pm-12.15am** Ⓥ

BUTTES AUX CAILLES & CHINATOWN

Dozens of East Asian restaurants line the main streets of Paris' Chinatown (13e), including av de Choisy and av d'Ivry (2, J11). But there are a couple of French options too. The cheapest *menus*, which go for about €8, are usually available only at lunch on weekdays.

L'Avant-Goût
(2, J10) $$
Modern French

In this prototype of the Parisian 'neo-bistro', chef Christophe Beaufront serves some of the most inventive modern cuisine around. Try the exquisitely tender seven-hour wild boar with crunchy polenta. Bookings essential. *Menu* €10/23.

✉ **26 rue Bobillot, 13e**

☎ **01 53 80 24 00**
Ⓜ **Place d'Italie**
🕐 **Tues-Sat noon-2pm, 8-11pm**

Le Temps des Cérises
(2, J10) $
French

The relaxed atmosphere of this 'anarchist' restaurant run by a workers' cooperative, together with the good solid fare (rabbit with mus-

tard, steak frites) and especially the low prices, keep regulars coming back for more. It's always packed and the atmosphere is great. *Menu* €10/20.

✉ **18-20 rue de la Buttes aux Cailles, 13e**
☎ **01 45 89 69 48**
Ⓜ **Corvisart**
🕐 **Mon-Fri 11.45am-2.15pm, Mon-Sat 7.30-11.45pm**

CHAMPS ÉLYSÉES

Few places along touristy ave des Champs Élysées offer good value, but some of the restaurants in the surrounding area are excellent.

Asian (3, C3) $$
Asian
Good Asian cooking is still something of a rarity in Paris. Loyal devotees flock to this restaurant for the fresh and piquant style, with influences ranging from Thai to Japanese. Bookings are advisable. Lunch *menu* €15.
✉ 30 av George V, 8e
☎ 01 56 89 11 00
Ⓜ George V ◷ noon-3pm, 7pm-1am

Le Bistrot du Sommelier
(3, A6) $$$$
French
This the Parisian restaurant *sans pareil* for wine buffs. Philippe Faure-Brac was named Meilleur Sommelier du Monde in 1992, and the *dégustation menus* offer his hand-picked selection of *crus* by-the-glass

matched with some canny cooking. Bookings essential; smart dress. *Menu* €60/75/100.
✉ 97 blvd Haussmann, 8e ☎ 01 42 65 24 85
Ⓜ St-Augustin
◷ Mon-Fri noon-2.30pm & 7.30-10.30pm

Elliott (3, A5) $$
American
With its sepia photos of baseball legends and moleskin-upholstered benches, you could almost be in a Frank Capra film. Eggs benedict washed down with Copperidge chardonnay is a lunch favourite. There are clairvoyant readings on Fri and Sat evenings and a DJ on Thurs evening. Lunch bookings essential.
✉ 166, blvd Haussmann
☎ 01 42 89 30 50
Ⓜ St-Philippe du-Roule
◷ Mon-Sat noon-3pm

& 8pm-2.30am, Sun noon-5pm

Flora Danica
(3, B3) $$$
Scandinavian
Just a few steps away from the bustle of the Champs Élysées is a quiet little terrace with a Nordic cast. Danish salmon is the speciality of the house, appearing in a multitude of guises: marinated, grilled, pickled or even fondue. Or try the reindeer fillets with wild berries – and try not to think of Christmas. Bookings advisable; smart dress. *Menu* €26.
✉ 142 av des Champs Élysées, 8e
☎ 01 44 13 86 26
Ⓜ Charles de Gaulle-Étoile
◷ Mon-Fri noon-2.30pm & 7.15-11pm, Sat-Sun noon-11pm

Whirling Champ Élysées waiters making dervish with your dinner.

Ladurée (3, B4) $$$
Afternoon Tea
The salons of this sumptuous *belle époque* tearoom, established in 1862, are named after the mistresses of Napoleon III: Mathilde, Castiglione and Paeva. But it's difficult to imagine any of them being as sweet as the pastries Ladurée is famous for. Mixed salads and light lunches round out the menu. Bookings advisable. Dinner *menu* €30.
✉ 75 ave des Champs Élysées, 8e
☎ 01 40 75 08 75
Ⓜ George V
⊘ 7.30am-1am Ⓥ

Maison Prunier (3, B2) $$$$
Seafood
This venerable fish and seafood restaurant, founded in 1925, is famed for its over-the-top Art Deco interior, as well as for its oysters and market-fresh catches of the day. Finish at the bar with one of a selection of vintage rums from Martinique. Book at least two days ahead.
✉ 16 av Victor Hugo, 16e ☎ 01 44 17 35 85
Ⓜ Charles de Gaulle-Étoile ⊘ Tues-Sat noon-3pm, Mon-Sat 7.30-11pm

Spoon Food & Wine (3, C4) $$$
International
Michelin 3-star chef Alain Ducasse invites diners to mix and match their own mains and sauces: do you prefer satay, curry or Béarnaise sauce with your grilled calamari? Controversially, the cellar features wines from the USA, Australia and Europe, with only a small proportion being French. Bookings necessary.
✉ 14 rue de Marignan, 8e ☎ 01 40 76 34 44
Ⓜ Franklin D Roosevelt ⊘ Mon-Fri noon-2pm & 7-11pm

GRANDS BOULEVARDS

This area, encompassing part of the 2e and 9e, has a number of fine restaurants worth trying. Neon-lit blvd du Montmartre (3, B10) and nearby parts of rue du Faubourg Montmartre (neither of which are anywhere near the neighbourhood of Montmartre) are one of Paris' most animated cafe and dining districts.

La Fermette d'Olivier (3, A10) $
Organic
Funky little organic/vegetarian eatery with a miniscule courtyard. Don't go past the *assiette zen*: a mixture of grains (bulghur, rice, semolina, buckwheat) with vegies and fish fillet, followed by the *tarte zen* (prune tart sprinkled with coconut) washed down with homemade apple juice.
✉ 40 rue du Faubourg-Montmartre, 9e
☎ 01 47 70 06 88
Ⓜ Grands Boulevards
⊘ Mon-Fri noon-3pm & 7-10pm Ⓥ

Mi Ranchito (3, A11) $$
Colombian
Of all Colombian exports, cuisine must be one of the rarest. In this small, discreet eatery the Andes meets the Antilles, with plantain

bananas, avocados, manioc, corn cakes, chilli and coconut milk among the exotic offerings. Dishes are based around chicken, seafood and beef, with some dishes cooked in banana leaves. Bookings advisable. Lunch *menu* €10, dinner and weekends €16.
✉ 35 rue de Montholon, 9e ☎ 01 48 78 45 94
Ⓜ Cadet ⊘ Sun-Fri noon-2.30pm, daily 7-midnight ♿

Le Phénix (3, B11) $$
French
Behind the 100-year old facade aproned-waiters cater to lovers of genuine *bistrot* fare: *saucisson lyonnaise* (boiled Lyon sausage with warm potatoes and shallots), *selle d'agneau à la provençale* (Provence-style saddle of lamb), *truffade* (potato cake with

Cantal cheese) or pigs' trotters with a spicy vinaigrette.
✉ 44 rue du Faubourg Poissonnière, 10e
☎ 01 47 70 35 40
Ⓜ Bonne Nouvelle
⊘ Mon-Fri noon-3pm & 7.30-11.30pm

Wally le Saharien (3, A10) $$$
Morocco
Wally's is a cut above most of the Maghreb restaurants in Paris, offering couscous in its pure Saharan form – without stock or vegetables, just a finely cooked grain served with a delicious sauce. The rich Moorish coffee is a fitting finish. Bookings advisable on Fri and Sat for dinner.
✉ 36 rue Rodier, 9e
☎ 01 42 85 51 90
Ⓜ St-Georges ⊘ Tues-Sat noon-2.30pm & 7.30-10.30pm Ⓥ

ÎLE ST-LOUIS

Famed for its ice cream as much as anything else, the Île St-Louis (4e) is generally an expensive place to eat. It's best suited to those looking for a light snack or the finest ingredients for lunch beside the Seine.

Brasserie de l'Île St-Louis (5, D6) **$$**
Alsatian
Founded in 1870, this spectacularly situated brasserie features *choucroute garnie* (sauerkraut with assorted prepared meats) and other Alsatian dishes, but you can also enjoy the location by just ordering coffee or a mug of beer. Bookings advisable.
✉ **55 Quai de Bourbon, 4e** ☎ **01 43 54 02 59**

Ⓜ **Pont Marie**
🕐 **Thurs-Tues 11.30am-1am (Thurs from 6pm)**

Les Fous de L'Île (5, E6) **$$**
French
An exception to the touristy nature of the Île St-Louis, this friendly and down-to-earth establishment serves reasonably priced light lunches and meals. Bookings advisable.
✉ **33 rue des Deux**

Noshing with Nippers

Unfortunately, French restaurants have yet to cotton onto the fact that children are diners too. Most restaurants don't have highchairs, children's menus or children's portions. In fact, children are rarely seen in most Parisian restaurants – which may help to explain the popularity of the American chain restaurants and their French counterparts (such as Hippopotamus) which specifically cater to parents with kids in tow.

Ponts, 4e
☎ **01 43 25 76 67**
Ⓜ **Pont Marie** 🕐 **Tues-Fri noon-11pm, Sat 3-11pm, Sun noon-7pm**

Isami (5, D5) **$$**
Japanese
A somewhat odd location for a wasabi hit, Isami has a reputation as one of the best sushi bars in the capital. The *joh sushi moriawase* is a comprehensive assortment of raw fish and seafood accompanied by rice, or try the *ika-natto* for a distinctive taste of Japan.
✉ **4 Quai d'Orléans**
☎ **01 40 46 06 97**
Ⓜ **Pont Marie**
🕐 **Tues-Sat noon-2pm, Tues-Sun 7-10pm**

Island dining

Simon Bracken

LOUVRE & LES HALLES

The area between the Forum des Halles and the Centre Pompidou (1er and western 4e) is filled with scores of cheap restaurants. Streets with places to eat include rue des Lombards, and bar- and bistro-lined rue Montorgueil.

L'Absinthe (3, C9) **$$$**
French
A young, energetic team run this classy bistro in the heart of the financial district, and close to Opéra. Servings are generous and presented with flair, and there's an extensive list of quality wines. The menu changes regularly or choose a daily special like lamb braised with cabbage. Reservations advisable. *Menu €25/30.*
✉ **24 Place du Marché, 1er ☎ 01 49 26 90 04** Ⓜ **Tuileries, Pyramides** ⊙ **Mon-Fri noon-2.15pm, Mon-Sat 7.30-11pm**

After the Louvre there's Café Marly.

Simon Bracken

Angelina (3, D8) **$$**
Afternoon Tea
Angelina's is where Louvre-weary tourists bump shoulders with trendy shoppers and coiffed matrons. It's true that some do partake of tea or munch a salad or sandwich, but the real reason they congregate here is the hot chocolate to die for.
✉ **226 rue de Rivoli, 1er ☎ 01 42 60 82 00** Ⓜ **Tuileries** ⊙ **9am-7pm** Ⓥ

Café Marly (3, E9) **$$$**
Modern French
Sipping something cool under the colonnades of the Louvre, overlooking the glowing pyramid on a warm spring evening … this is about as good as it gets. The Marly serves fresh and contemporary fare, tending towards white meats, fish and salad, with a great fruit salad to finish. Bookings advisable.
✉ **93 rue de Rivoli, 1er ☎ 01 49 26 06 60** Ⓜ **Palais Royal** ⊙ **11am-1am**

L'Épicerie (3, D11) **$$**
French
Features fresh food from the nearby food wholesale, simply and deliciously prepared. The *velouté de potiron* (pumpkin soup) is flavoursome and creamy, and the *confit de canard* perfectly balances crunchy skin with melt-in-your-mouth meat.
✉ **30 rue Montorgueil, 1er ☎ 01 40 28 49 78**

Ⓜ **Les Halles, Etienne Marcel** ⊙ **Mon-Sat noon-3pm, Mon-Sun 7.30pm-midnight**

Joe Allen (5, A7) **$$**
American
This friendly American bar/restaurant has a great atmosphere and a good selection of Californian wines. Snack on buffalo wings or tuck into a grilled half chicken with barbecue sauce, baked potato and coleslaw. Sunday brunch is noon-4pm. *Menu €18/20.*
✉ **30 rue Pierre Lescot, 1er ☎ 01 42 36 70 13** Ⓜ **Étienne Marcel** ⊙ **noon-2am**

La Mousson (3, D9) **$**
Cambodian
A warm and friendly oasis in a *quartier* known for its cold beauty. Try the spicy *bo* buns, tender chicken with basil, or the house speciality, *nun bachok* curry – a delicious cocktail of rice vermicelli, chicken and crab in a thick curry sauce.
✉ **9 rue Thérèse, 1er ☎ 01 42 96 67 76** Ⓜ **Palais Royal, Pyramides** ⊙ **noon-2.30pm & 7.30-10.30pm**

Wasabi (3, D12) **$$**
Japanese
Good-value takeaway or sit-down stop for sushi, yakitori and miso soup.
✉ **93 blvd de Sébastopol, 2e ☎ 01 40 26 44 78** Ⓜ **Réaumur Sébastopol** ⊙ **Mon-Sat 10am-10.30pm**

MARAIS & ST-PAUL

One of Paris' premier neighbourhoods for eating out is the Marais (3e and 4e), whose atmospheric, narrow streets are filled with small eateries and bars of every imaginable kind.

404 (5, A8) $$$
Moroccan
The 404 has some of the best couscous and *tajine* in Paris. It also has excellent grills and tasty aniseed bread. The restaurant – done up like the inside of an old Moroccan home – is owned by the French-Arab comedian Smaïn, so the atmosphere is always upbeat. The Sunday *brunch berbère* (Berber brunch) is recommended. Bookings essential. Lunch *menu* €14, weekend brunch *menu* €19.
✉ 69 rue des Gravilliers, 3e ☎ 01 42 74 57 81 Ⓜ Arts et Métiers ⊘ noon-2.30pm (Sat-Sun to 4pm), 8pm-midnight

Amadeo (5, D7) $$
Modern French
This chic Mozart-mad restaurant is decidedly gay, although straight diners are also very welcome. The food is stylish and delicious. A highlight is the live opera or operetta performance held on the first Thurs of each month, with a special *prix fixe menu* to

match. Bookings essential. Lunch *menu* €12/14.
✉ 19 rue François Miron, 4e
☎ 01 48 87 01 02
Ⓜ St-Paul, Hôtel de Ville
⊘ Mon-Fri lunch & dinner, Sat dinner

Baracane (5, E8) $$
French
Bustling family-run bistro specialising in southwestern provincial cuisine, just around the corner from the Places des Vosges. The *magret de canard* (fillet of duck breast) is recommended.
✉ 38 rue des Tournelles, 4e
☎ 01 42 71 43 33
Ⓜ Chemin Vert
⊘ Mon-Sat noon-2.30pm & 7pm-midnight

Café Beaubourg (5, B7) $$
French
This minimalist cafe opposite the Centre Pompidou draws an arty crowd, and there's always free entertainment on the large square in front. Sunday

brunch on the terrace is highly recommended.
✉ 100 rue St-Martin, 1er ☎ 01 48 87 63 96
Ⓜ Châtelet-Les Halles
⊘ Mon-Fri 8am-1am, Sat-Sun 8am-2am

Chez Marianne (5, D7) $$
Kosher
A Sephardic (Middle Eastern/North African Jewish) alternative to the nearby Ashkenazic (Eastern European Jewish) **Jo Goldenberg**, this restaurant/deli/takeaway specialises in *mezze* (felafel, hummus, meatballs etc), as well as honey-oozing baklava. Bookings advisable. *Menu* €10/13.
✉ 2 rue des Hospitalières St-Gervais, 4e ☎ 01 42 72 18 86
Ⓜ St-Paul
⊘ 11am-midnight

L'Enoteca (5, E7) $$$
Italian
Great Italian food to accompany a list of over 300 excellent Italian wines. Risotto with gorgonzola and pears, tagliatelle with prawns and

In Vino Veritas

Alcoholic drinks are available wherever you eat, or at cafes even if you don't eat. Many French diners will have *un kir* (a white wine flavoured with blackcurrant syrup), a glass of champagne (*une coupe*), or a beer (*une pression*) as an aperitif, and then wine with their meal. Wine with meals generally starts at around €13 a bottle, with most being in the €16-24 range; €40 will get you a fine drop indeed. A selection of wines are always available by the glass (*un verre*, €3-4) or jug (*un pichet*, €6-10 depending on size).

asparagus, and carpaccio with rocket are among the favourites. Bookings advisable. Lunch menu €16.

✉ 25 rue Charles V, 4e
☎ 01 42 78 91 44
Ⓜ Pont Marie
🕐 Mon-Fri noon-2pm, Mon-Sat 7.30-10.30pm

Ma Bourgogne
(5, E8) $$$
French
Overlooking Place des Vosges, this is one of the few Parisian eateries where you can eat on the terrace day and night seven days a week. Menu €30.

✉ 19 Place des Vosges, 4e ☎ 01 42 78 44 64
Ⓜ St-Paul, Bastille
🕐 8am-1.30am

Pitchi Poï (5, E7) $$
Polish
This Eastern European

Jewish restaurant will warm the cockles with its trademark tchoulent (slow-simmered duck with vegetables) or datcha (smoked salmon served with a baked spud and cream). And of course there's chopped liver and strudel. Bookings advisable for dinner. Menu €19.

✉ 7 Place du Marché Ste-Catherine, 4e
☎ 01 42 77 46 15
Ⓜ St-Paul 🕐 noon-2.30pm & 7.30-11pm ♿

Le Réconfort (5, C9) $$
French
Had enough of cheek-by-jowl dining? The 'Comfort' has generous space between tables, is quiet enough to chat without yelling, and turns out some very tasty dishes from the home-made foie gras to the glace au gingembre

(ginger ice cream).
✉ 37 rue de Poitou
☎ 01 42 76 06 36
Ⓜ Filles du Calvaire
🕐 Mon-Sat noon-2pm & 8-11pm

Robert et Louise
(5, C8) $$
French
This authentic country inn – complete with red gingham curtains – offers delightful, unfussy and inexpensive French food prepared by a husband and wife team. Dishes include côte de bœuf roasted on an open fire. Bookings advisable in the evenings; cash only.

✉ 64 rue Vieille du Temple, 3e
☎ 01 42 78 55 89
Ⓜ St-Sébastien Froissart
🕐 Mon-Sat noon-2.30pm & 7-10pm

Je Suis Végétarien

Vegetarians are a near-invisible minority in France. Exclusively vegetarian eateries are rare, though many places have at least one veggie dish on the menu (but you'll soon get sick of cheese omelettes) and you can get a fresh salad just about anywhere.

Most North African and Middle Eastern restaurants have some meatless dishes on the menu. Better still, there's a handful of Indian restaurants to choose from. **Passage Brady** (3, B13) in the 10e is chock-full of subcontinental restaurants and groceries. Elsewhere, **La Ville de Jagannath** (2, E12; ☎ 01 43 55 80 81) at 101 rue St-Maur, 11e, is a New Age-inspired thali spot, while **L'Étoile du Kasmir** (2, F12; ☎ 01 43 55 57 60) at 63 rue de Charonne, 11e, does filling, inexpensive thali lunches.

Unfortunately, very few fixed-price menus include vegetarian options. A couple of places where vegetarians can find a decent meal are:

Aquarius (p. 80)– good-value vegetarian restaurant
Les Quatre et Une Saveurs (p. 84) – macrobiotic dishes
Jardin des Pâtes (p. 83) – not a vegetarian restaurant, but there's a good selection of meatless dishes on the menu
La Verte Tige (5, D9; ☎ 01 42 78 19 90) 13 rue Ste-Anastase, 3e – inventive, meatless Iranian cuisine
La Victoire Suprême du Cœur (5, A6; ☎ 01 40 41 93 95) 41 rue des Bourdonnais, 1er – Sri Chimnoy centre serving decent vegetarian fare

Simon Bracken

MONTMARTRE & PIGALLE

This is a popular nightlife district. The restaurants along rue des Trois Frères, 18e (4, D6), are a much better bet than their touristy counterparts around Place du Tertre. Many are open seven days a week, but only for dinner.

L'Auberge du Clou
(2, C9) **$$**
French
Open since the late 19th century, traces remain of an original fresco by Toulouse-Lautrec in the cellar. The food combines excellent country cooking with inventive, cosmopolitan flavours. The set menu changes weekly (€12/15). Dishes range from Galician-style octopus to artichoke heart with warm foie gras and sautéed pork with clams.
✉ **30 ave de Trudaine**
☎ **01 48 78 22 48**
Ⓜ **Pigalle, Anvers**
🕑 **Tues-Sat noon-2pm & 7.30-11.30pm**

Au Bon Coin (2, B9) **$**
French
This unpretentious neighbourhood bar and restaurant has been in the family for three generations. The lunch menu offers simple dishes with fresh market produce. Ask patron Jean-Louis to recommend the perfect drop of wine to complement it. No reservations.
✉ **49 rue des Cloÿs, 18e**
☎ **01 46 06 91 36**
Ⓜ **Jules Joffrin**
🕑 **restaurant: Mon-Sat noon-3pm; bar: Mon-Fri 7-9.30pm, Sat 8am-3pm**

La Mascotte (4, C4) **$**
French
Specialising in seafood and charcuterie, this unassuming little bar/restaurant is an

Would You Like Smoke with That?

Smoke is an unpleasant fact of life in cramped French restaurants. In fact, Parisians smoke anywhere, anytime – irrespective of no-smoking signs or the comfort of others (except in cinemas and on public transport). Even many non-smokers will defend the right of smokers to light up whenever they feel the urge.

No smoking rules and spaces simply don't work. You can try complaining – but don't (or perhaps *do*) hold your breath. If you absolutely can't abide smoke, sit upwind on a terrace.

Peppe La Plume

excellent spot to sample oysters, mussels, fish crab and lobster. Bookings advisable. *Menu* €12/13/24.
✉ **52 rue des Abbesses, 18e** ☎ **01 46 06 28 15**
Ⓜ **Abbesses**
🕑 **Tues-Sun 7am-1am**

Le Taroudant
(4, D4) **$$**
Moroccan
Discreetly tucked away in the *bon vivant* Abbesses quarter, this traditional Moroccan restaurant satisfies from the genial welcome from the patron to the freshness, lightness and value of its tasty *tajines* and couscous. Try a drop from the remarkable North African wine list. Bookings advisable.
✉ **8 rue Aristide Bruant, 18e** ☎ **01 42 64 95 81**
Ⓜ **Abbesses, Blanche**
🕑 **Thurs-Tues 11am-3pm & 6.30pm-midnight** **V**

MONTPARNASSE

Since the 1920s, the area around blvd du Montparnasse (6e and 14e) has been one of the city's premier avenues for enjoying that most Parisian of pastimes: sitting in a cafe and checking out the passers-by.

Aquarius (2, H7) $
Vegetarian
The best of Paris' few vegetarian restaurants, Aquarius offers an imaginative and filling range of dishes for both committed vegans and vegos as well as those simply craving something a little less 'sophisticated' than much French cuisine. There's a second Aquarius (5, C7; ☎ 01 48 87 48 71) at 54 rue Ste-Croix de la Bretonnerie, 4e (Ⓜ Rambuteau). Bookings advisable. Lunch *menu* €10.
✉ **40 rue de Gergovie, 14e** ☎ **01 45 41 36 88** Ⓜ **Plaisance, Pernéty** ⏲ **Mon-Sat noon-2.30pm & 7-10.30pm** Ⓥ

La Cagouille (2, H8) $$$
Seafood
Chef Gérard Allemandou gets rave reviews for his fish and shellfish dishes at this pleasant cafe/restaurant with its terrace for lunch alfresco. Bookings essential. *Menu* €23/39.
✉ **10-12 Place Constantin Brancusi, 14e** ☎ **01 43 22 09 01** Ⓜ **Gaîté** ⏲ **noon-2.30pm & 7.30-10.30pm**

Le Caméléon (3, K8) $$
French
Not far from the big names of the blvd Montparnasse, this quaint little place does a nice 'nouveau' bistro turn in a traditional setting. Lobster ravioli is a favourite among the loyal *habitués*, and the Auvergne sausage with *purée maison* is a perfect French rendition of bangers and mash. Bookings advisable. Lunch *menu* €19.
✉ **6 rue de Chevreuse, 6e** ☎ **01 43 20 63 43** Ⓜ **Vavin** ⏲ **Mon-Fri noon-2pm, Mon-Sat 8-10.30pm**

Dix Vins (3, J6) $
French
Size isn't everything: this tiny place exudes quality with an emphasis on some excellent vintage wines to accompany *boudin noir* (black pudding) or *cannette rôtie sauce au poivre* (roast duckling with pepper sauce). Set *menu* €16.
✉ **57 rue Falguière, 15e** ☎ **01 43 20 91 77** Ⓜ **Pasteur** ⏲ **Tues-Sat noon-2.30pm, Mon-Sat 8-11pm**

Monsieur Lapin (2, H8) $$$
French
What's up doc? At least half a dozen different ways of preparing Mr Bunny, that's what. But it's not all rabbit, there's also an impressive range of seafood (eg warm oysters in champagne) and other meat dishes – all prepared and served with admirable care and attention. Bookings advisable. *Menu* €28.
✉ **11 rue Raymond Losserand, 14e** ☎ **01 43 20 21 39** Ⓜ **Gaîté** ⏲ **Wed-Sun noon-2pm, Tues-Sun 7.30-11pm**

Menu v. Menu

Most restaurants offer you the choice of ordering à la carte (from the menu) or ordering one fixed-price, multi-course meal known in French as a *menu* or a *formule*. The latter usually has fewer choices but allows you to pick two out of three courses (eg starter and main course or main course and dessert). A *menu* almost always costs much less than ordering à la carte. Where we have indicated more than one *menu* price, the cheaper is normally only available at lunchtime.

Note that the word 'menu' is one of the 'false friends' of English and French. If you really want to see the menu (ie a list of all the dishes available) you ask for *la carte*.

Simon Bracken

ODÉON & ST-GERMAIN

Rue St-André des Arts (5, B4) is lined with restaurants, including a few down the covered passage between Nos 59 and 61. There are lots of places between Église St-Sulpice and Église St-Germain des Prés (5, A3), especially along rue des Canettes, rue Princesse and rue Guisarde.

Chez Albert (5, A4) $$$
Portuguese
Authentic Portuguese food is not easy to come by in Paris, but this friendly family-run place has it in spades: *cataplana* (pork with clams), numerous *bacalhau* (dried cod) dishes and prawns sautéed in lots of garlic, plus a good selection of Portuguese wines. Bookings advisable. *Menu* €15/18.
✉ 43 rue Mazarine, 6e
☎ 01 46 33 22 57
Ⓜ Odéon
🕐 Tues-Sat noon-2.30pm, Mon-Sat 7-11.30pm

La Cigale (3, G7) $$
French
More than just hot air, chef Gérard Idoux has been Paris' undisputed soufflé master for seven years. Depending on season you can choose between 60 and 80 savoury or sweet soufflés – mushroom, sea urchin, pumpkin, or apricot for dessert.
✉ 11bis rue Chomel
☎ 01 45 48 87 87
Ⓜ Sèvres Babylone
🕐 Mon-Fri noon-2.30pm, Mon-Sat 7.30-11pm

Coffee Parisien (5, A3) $
American
This cafe/diner offers something of a détente in the burger-chain wars. Surrounded by Ameri-kitsch and under the ever-present eye of JFK, shining, happy

Simon Bracken

Les Deux Cafes
Side by side on blvd St-Germain sit **Les Deux Magots** (No 170; at left) and **Café de Flore** (No 172), once the canteens of bohemian artists and writers such as Jean-Paul Sartre, Simone de Beauvoir and Albert Camus. Today they cater for a more prosaic clientele, but their terraces are still a good spot to watch the passing parade in style.

people munch commendable cheeseburgers, club sandwiches, Caesars and other snacky offerings late into the night.
✉ 4 rue Princesse, 6e
☎ 01 43 54 18 18
Ⓜ Mabillon
🕐 11.30am-midnight

Cour de Rohan (5, B4) $$
Afternoon Tea
Local writers and publishers seek peace, quiet and home-made scones in this slightly faded tearoom, with its assortment of exquisite furniture and *objets*. Mixed salads and daily specials complement the aromatic teas, while three pastry chefs keep the dessert cart piled with delicious delicacies.
✉ 59-61 rue St-André des Arts, 6e
☎ 01 43 25 79 67

Ⓜ Mabillon, Odéon
🕐 noon-7.30pm (to 11pm Sat-Sun) V

Jacques Cagna (5, B4) $$$$
French
In his 17th-century mansion hung with Flemish masters, Jacques Cagna continues his mastery of original haute cuisine – *filet de bœuf poêlé aux truffes de Périgord* or escalope of veal sweetbreads with crayfish and fresh coriander lasagne. The €40 lunch *menu* (€70 dinner) is a fine introduction to the man's great talents. Bookings advisable.
✉ 14 rue des Grands Augustins, 6e
☎ 01 43 26 49 39
Ⓜ Mabillon, Odéon
🕐 Tues-Fri noon-2pm, Mon-Sat 7.30-10.30pm

Le Petit Zinc (3, F9) $$$
French
This lovely (and expensive) place serves regional southwest French specialities (the signature calf's liver is sublime) in mock-Art Nouveau splendour. Bookings advisable. Menu €26.
✉ 11 rue St-Benoît, 6e
☎ 01 42 61 20 60
Ⓜ St-Germain des Prés
🕐 noon-2am

Polidor (5, C3) $
French
Lunch at this very cosy *crêmerie-restaurant* is a trip back to Victor Hugo's Paris – the restaurant and its decor

date from 1845. The inexpensive *menus* (€9/17) of tasty, family-style French cuisine attract students, locals and tourists alike. Specialities include the most famous *tarte tatin* (caramelised apple pie) in Paris. Cash only.
✉ 41 rue Monsieur-le-Prince, 6e
☎ 01 43 26 95 34
Ⓜ Odéon
🕐 noon-2.30pm & 7pm-12.30am (Sun to 11pm)

Le Télégraphe (3, E8) $$$
French
Great atmosphere and

sumptuous cuisine is served up at Le Télégraphe located in a Belle Époque residence. Its soaring high ceilings and gorgeous mosaics have been faithfully conserved. Plates are lovingly and attractively presented: *carpaccio de foie gras*, *bavette d'aloyau* (fillet of veal) and baked pear with caramel are all wonderfully delicious. Menu €30. Reservations advisable.
✉ 41 rue de Lille
☎ 01 42 92 03 04
Ⓜ Rue-du-Bac
🕐 Mon-Fri noon-2.30pm, Mon-Sat 7.30pm-midnight

OBERKAMPF & BELLEVILLE

The northern part of the 11e, east of Place de la République, and the 20e along rue Oberkampf and its extension, rue de Ménilmontant, are increasingly popular with diners and denizens of the night. Rue de Belleville (2, D13) is dotted with Chinese, Vietnamese and Turkish places, and blvd de Belleville has loads of kosher couscous restaurants (closed on Saturday).

Le Baratin (2, D13) $$
French
This animated wine bistro, just a step away from a stunning vista over Paris and the lively Belleville quarter, offers some of the best food in the 20e. The wine selection (by the glass or carafe) is excellent. Bookings advisable. Weekday lunch *menu* €12.
✉ 3 rue Jouye-Rouve, 20e ☎ 01 43 49 39 70

Ⓜ Belleville
🕐 restaurant: Tues-Fri & Sun 11-3pm, Tues-Sun 6-11.30pm; bar: 11-2am

Le Charbon (2, E12) $
French
With its remarkable distressed-retro-industrial ambience, the Charbon was the first – and many opine the best – of the hip cafes and bars to sprout up

in Ménilmontant. Its cocktail of frenetic cool, inexpensive *plats du jour* and evening DJs or live music still hits the spot.
✉ 109 rue Oberkampf, 11e ☎ 01 43 57 55 13
Ⓜ Parmentier
🕐 9am-2am

Juan et Juanita (2, E12) $$
French
The purple and green New Age decor perfectly complements a menu that balances grandma's cottage with the exotic: salads with subtle taste and colour combinations, a delicate lamb *tajine* with apricots, tenderloin of pork with horseradish, mango soup with vanilla ice cream or baked figs with wine. Two-course

Food with a View
Café Marly (p. 76) is lovely at night with its view of the Louvre's pyramid; **Café Beaubourg** (p. 77) has a view of the Pompidou Centre. For panoramic views try the **teahouse** on the 9th floor of the Institut du Monde Arabe (p. 39), **Georges** atop the Centre Pompidou (p. 16), **La Terrasse** (p. 85), or **Altitude 95** or the **Jules Verne** on the Tour Eiffel (p. 33).

menu €14.

✉ 82 rue Jean-Pierre Timbaud, 11e
☎ 01 43 57 60 15
Ⓜ Parmentier, Couronnes
🕐 Tues-Fri 8pm-midnight, Sat-Sun 8pm-1am

Krung Thep (2, D12) $
Thai

Considered by many to be the most authentic Thai restaurant in Paris, the kitsch 'Bangkok' is a small (some might say cramped) place with favourites like green curries, tom yam gung and fish or chicken steamed in banana leaves. The steamed shrimp ravioli and stuffed crab also hit the spot. Bookings advisable.

✉ 93 rue Julien Lacroix, 20e ☎ 01 43 66 83 74
Ⓜ Belleville
🕐 6pm-midnight

Au Trou Normand (3, A15) $
French

This very French, cosy little canteen is famous for having some of the lowest prices in Paris. Diners sit at shared, plastic-covered tables, swigging house red from Pyrex glasses and tucking into simple but copious mounds of food. Mains are mostly meat with home-made frites. No reservations; cash only.

✉ 9 rue Jean-Pierre Timbaud, 11e
☎ 01 48 05 80 23
Ⓜ Oberkampf
🕐 Mon-Fri noon-2.30pm, Mon-Sat 7.30-11.30pm

QUARTIER LATIN

Chez Léna et Mimille (5, F2) $$$
French

The fabulous terrace of this cosy but elegant little place overlooks a lovely park with a burbling fountain. The food is tasty and inventive (leg of lamb with chorizo). Save room for the pears poached in wine with gingerbread ice cream. *Menus* €15/30.

✉ 32 rue Tournefort, 5e ☎ 01 47 07 72 47
Ⓜ Place Monge, Censier Daubenton 🕐 Tues-Fri noon-2.30pm, Mon-Sat 7.30-11pm

The Chipper (5, E3) $$
British

Shame on you! But, hey, we all need a cheap fix of chips, battered cod and mushy peas from time to time – even in Paris – and this is the real McCoy.

✉ 14 rue Thouin, 5e
☎ 01 43 26 05 55
Ⓜ Place Monge
🕐 noon-midnight

Fogon St-Julien (5, C5) $$$
Spanish

Come for the tapas and authentic paella (saffron, vegetable, rabbit, chicken or seafood). The best is the *arroz negro*, black with squid ink hiding chunks of fish, cuttlefish and shrimp. Bookings advisable. *Menu* €29.

✉ 10 rue St-Julien-le-Pauvre, 5e
☎ 01 43 54 31 33
Ⓜ Maubert-Mutualité, St-Michel 🕐 noon-2.30pm & 7pm-midnight

Jardin des Pâtes (3, J12) $
Italian

Not far from the Jardin des Plantes, the cosy 'Garden of Pastas' has as many types of pasta as you care to name (wholewheat, buckwheat, chestnut etc), all made from

Simon Bracken

Instant indigestion in the Quartier Latin

100% *biologique* (natural) stone-ground grains. The dishes are simple and filling. Wine by the glass and excellent fresh juices are available. Bookings advisable for dinner.

✉ **4 rue Lacépède, 5e**
☎ **01 43 31 50 71**
Ⓜ **Cardinal Lemoine**
🕑 **Tues-Sun noon-2.30pm & 7-11pm** **V**

Moissonnier (5, E5) **$$$**
Lyonnais
Hearty Lyon-inspired cuisine has been served at this elegant restaurant since 1960, including *quenelles* (a kind of fish dumpling), *saladier Lyonnais* (a selection of appetisers including fresh greens, bacon, eggs and anchovies), *boudin noir* (black pudding) and tripe. Bookings advisable. *Menu* €24.

✉ **28 rue des Fossés St-Bernard, 5e**
☎ **01 43 29 87 65**
Ⓜ **Cardinal Lemoine**
🕑 **Tues-Sun noon-1.30pm, Tues-Sat 7-9.30pm**

Les Quatre et Une Saveurs (5, E4) **$$**
Macrobiotic
Close to the picturesque Place de la Contrescarpe is one of Paris' few truly macrobiotic restaurants – all ingredients are fresh and certified 100% organic. Whet you appetite with *mü* tea (made from16 plants) before an *assiette complète de seitan* or the artistically presented *crudités* (white radishes pickled in plum vinegar, seaweed, beans, rice and millet). Set *menu* €30.

✉ **72 rue du Cardinal Lemoine, 5e**
☎ **01 43 26 88 80**
Ⓜ **Cardinal Lemoine**
🕑 **Tues-Sun noon-2.30pm & 7-10.30pm**
V

Restaurant du Hammam de la Mosquée (3, K13) **$**
Moroccan
The restaurant at this authentic – and very atmospheric – mosque and *hammam* serves the usual complement of *tajines* and couscous. For the complete experience, the *formule orientale* includes use of the *hammam* and a massage plus a meal for €50.

✉ **39 rue Geoffroy St-Hilaire, 5e**
☎ **01 43 31 38 20**
Ⓜ **Place Monge**
🕑 **12.30-3pm & 7.30-10.30pm**

Surveying the menu (or is that la carte?; see p. 80) on rue Mouffetard

Rob Flynn

TROCADERO & SOUTH

The 16e is one of the wealthiest and most *huppé* (posh) in Paris. Though there's precious little to do at night, there are a few exceptional (and very classy) restaurants that might tempt you to cross the river.

A&M le bistrot
(2, G2)   **$$**
French
The well-respected chefs of Apicius and Marius have joined talents in the bourgeois 16e, and are doing a fine trade in finely tuned modern bistro cuisine. Efficient service and impeccable presentation are what the besuited clientele demand and receive. Bookings advisable. *Menu* €26/32.
✉ **136 blvd Murat, 16e**
☎ **01 45 27 39 60**
Ⓜ **Port de St-Cloud**
🕒 **Mon-Fri noon-2.30pm, Mon-Sat 7.45-10.30pm**

La Gare **(2, F4)**   **$$**
French
The platforms and tracks in this converted train station have been replaced with an open kitchen and tables, resulting in a spacious, light, welcoming and *branché* brasserie at the chic end of town. The speciality of the house is poultry *à la rôtisserie*, perfectly cooked and well presented. Bookings advisable at weekends.
✉ **19 Chausée de la Muette, 16e** ☎ **01 42 15 15 31** Ⓜ **La Muette**
🕒 **restaurant: noon-3pm, 7pm-midnight; bar: 5.30pm-midnight**

La Plage Parisienne
(2, G4)   **$$**
French
You don't have to worry about sand in your meal at this 'Parisian Beach', under the beautiful Pont Mirabeau. The magnificent wood and glass structures, extended by a renovated barge and an open summer deck, are the perfect place to escape the streets for a light lunch or summer dinner. Bookings advisable. *Menu* €40; children's weekend *menu* €16.
✉ **Port de Javel Haut, 15e** ☎ **01 40 59 41 00**
Ⓜ **Javel, Mirabeau**
🕒 **noon-2.30pm & 8-11pm** ♿

La Terrasse **(3, C2) $$$**
French/German
Elegant dishes (venison, seafood) complement the sublime panoramic views of the capital (Arc de Triomphe, Eiffel Tour, Sacré Cœur) from this top-floor restaurant not far from L'Étoile. Service is friendly and unfussed. Reservations advisable.
✉ **30 rue Galilée, 16e**
☎ **01 47 20 51 51**
Ⓜ **Boissière** 🕒 **Mon-Fri 9am-3.30pm, Tues-Sat 6.30pm-10.30pm**

Le Totem **(3, E1)**   **$$**
French
The famous faces at the bar, the spectacular views of the Tour Eiffel and the imaginative and satisfying dishes are just a few of the delights of the *très, très branché* Totem. Bookings not accepted in summer. *Menu* €20.
✉ **Musée de l'Homme, 17 Place du Trocadéro, 16e** ☎ **01 47 27 28 29**
Ⓜ **Trocadéro**
🕒 **noon-11.30pm**

Coffee Primer
un café – a single shot of espresso
une noisette – a shot of espresso with a spot of milk
un café crème – a shot of espresso lengthened with steamed milk (closest thing to a caffè latte)
un café allongé – an espresso lengthened with hot water (closest thing to American-style coffee)

Simon Bracken

WORTH A TRIP

Le Pavillon Puebla
(2, C12) **$$$**
Catalan
This exquisite Catalan restaurant is housed in a Second Empire pavilion in Buttes Chaumont. The seafood and fish dishes – anchovy *tarte, bouilla-baisse,* and cod stuffed with snails – are as attractive as the wonderful terrace (open in summer). For dessert, don't miss the *millefeuille aux fraises* (strawberries in layers of flaky pastry). Bookings advisable. *Menu* €29/39.
✉ **Parc des Buttes Chaumont, cnr ave Simon Bolivar and rue Botzaris, 19e**
☎ **01 42 08 92 62**
Ⓜ **Buttes Chaumont**
◷ **Tues-Sat noon-2.30pm, 7.30-10.30pm**

L'Homme Bleu
(2, E12) **$$**
North African
Feast on Berber delicacies under an authentic Tuareg tent or in the Moroccan-style vaulted cellar, including a delicate *tajine* combining prunes, pears, almonds, orange and cinnamon or a simple chicken *pastilla* sealed in a light fritter. Dessert: a platter of pasties or almonds, pistachios, honey and orange blossoms.
✉ **55bis rue Jean-Pierre Timbaud, 11e**
☎ **01 48 07 05 63**
Ⓜ **Parmentier**
◷ **Mon-Sat 5pm-2am**

La Régalade (2, J8) **$$**
French
The *plat du jour* of this unpretentious bistro is the culinary talent of chef Yves Camdeborde. The *menu* might include a salt-cod gazpacho with hot-tomato sorbet or veal kidneys with almonds and a juniper-flavoured sauce. Bookings essential. *Menu* €30.
✉ **49 ave Jean-Moulin, 14e** ☎ **01 45 45 68 58**
Ⓜ **Alésia**
◷ **Tues-Fri noon-2pm, Tues-Sat 7pm-midnight**

Le Zéphyr (2, D13) **$$**
French
Out in the sticks beyond Buttes Chaumont, this elegant 1930s bistro is worth the trip for its refined cooking and genial ambience. A typical *menu* offers eggplant ravioli with mint vinaigrette and roasted lamb noisettes with anchovies and *crème brûlée à la tomate* to finish. Bookings advisable. *Menu* €12/26.
✉ **1 rue du Jourdain, 20e** ☎ **01 46 36 65 81**
Ⓜ **Jourdain**
◷ **Mon-Fri noon-2.30pm, Mon-Sat 8-11pm**

Food Markets
Paris' food markets – whether temporary or permanent – offer some of the choicest comestibles on the planet, and are an experience not to be missed. They are generally open Tues-Sat 8am-1pm and Sun 8am-1pm.

Place d'Aligre (2, G12) 12e Ⓜ Ledru Rollin
◷ mornings only
Blvd de Belleville (2, D12) 11e Ⓜ Belleville
◷ Tues & Fri
Rue de Buci (5, A3) 6e Ⓜ Mabillon
Blvd de la Chapelle (4, D9) 18e Ⓜ Barbés Rochechouart ◷ Wed & Sat
Rue Cler (3, F4) 7e Ⓜ École Militaire
Rue Daguerre (2, H8) 14e Ⓜ Denfert Rochereau
Rue Montorgueil (3, D11) 1er Ⓜ Les Halles
Rue Mouffetard (3, K12) 5e Ⓜ Censier Daubenton
Blvd Richard Lenoir (3, F15) 11e Ⓜ Bastille
◷ Sunday mornings

Simon Bracken

entertainment

Whether your musical tastes run to opera, jazz or house, or you prefer theatre, cinema or experimental dance, there's always way too much going on in Paris to ever get bored. The French take Culture (with a capital C) seriously, and they match this with investment in world-class performance spaces, support of creative companies and a general enthusiasm for both classical and fringe arts.

Paris must also rate as one of the best cities in the world for cinema, with around 300 films screening in any particular week, many in English with French subtitles. In addition to first-release English-language and French films, you'll find retrospectives of the great directors (Hitchcock is a perennial favourite) and some films from Africa, Asia and Eastern Europe.

Paris now has two great opera houses (Garnier and Bastille) and a rich opera season – though you need to book several months in advance by mail (see the following section for details) to ensure good seats.

Listings

It's virtually impossible to sample the richness of Paris' entertainment scene without first perusing the pages of *Pariscope* (**e** www.pariscope.fr), *L'Officiel des Spectacles* or *Zurban* (**e** www.zurban.com), all of which come out on Wednesday. *Pariscope* includes a five-page insert in English courtesy of *Time Out* weekly events magazine. For information on clubs and the music scene, magazines like *Les Inrockuptibles, LYLO* and *Nova* are particularly useful.

The city's music venues are legion, from enormous concert halls to poky (and smoky) little bars and jazz clubs. Keep an ear open for the regular classical music concerts held in many churches.

Today Sacré Cœur's steps, tomorrow Le Zénith.

SPECIAL EVENTS

January/February *La Grande Parade de Paris* – parade along the Grands Boulevards on New Year's Day

Chinese New Year – dragon parades and other festivities are held in Chinatown (13e) and rue Au Maire (3e)

March/April *Banlieues Bleues* – this jazz festival held in Saint Denis and other Paris suburbs attracts big-name talent

April *Marathon International de Paris* – mid-month; from Place de la Concorde (1er) to av Foch (16e)

May/June *Internationaux de France de Tennis* (French Open Tennis Tournament) – held in Stade Roland Garros

June *Gay Pride* – around 20 June; a colourful Saturday-afternoon parade through the Marais

Fête de la Musique – 21 June; featuring impromptu live performances all over the city

June/July *La Course des Garçons de Café* – hundreds of waiters and waitresses race through central Paris carrying a glass and a bottle balanced on a tray

July *La Goutte d'Or en Fête* – world music festival (rai, reggae, rap etc) at Place de Léon, 18e

Bastille Day – 14 July; *bals des sapeurs-pompiers* are held at fire stations (on the night of the 13th); fire brigade and military parade travels along the Champs Élysées (10am); a huge display of *feux d'artifice* (fireworks) either near the Tour Eiffel or at the Invalides (around 11pm)

Tour de France – 3rd or 4th Sun; the world's most prestigious cycling event ends on the Champs Élysées

September *Festival d'Automne* – begins Sept; Autumn Festival of music and theatre held throughout the city over three months

October *Foire Internationale d'Art Contemporain (FIAC)* – huge contemporary art fair with some 150 galleries represented

December *Christmas Eve Mass* – 24-25 Dec; midnight Mass is celebrated at many Paris churches, including Notre Dame

New Year's Eve – 31 Dec; festivities take place on blvd St-Michel (5e), Place de la Bastille (11e) and the Champs Élysées (8e)

Sally Dillon

THEATRE & COMEDY

Almost all of Paris' theatre productions are performed in French. There are a few English-speaking troupes around, though – look for ads on metro poster boards and in English-language periodicals (eg *FUSAC* – France USA Contacts).

Les Abbesses (4, D5)

The neoclassical home for the Théâtre de la Ville is the venue for mainly contemporary theatre, music and dance works.

✉ 31 rue des Abbesses, 18e ☎ 01 42 74 22 77
e www.theatre delaville-paris.com
Ⓜ Abbesses ☺ box office Tues-Sat 5-8pm
$ €15-30

Bouffes du Nord

(2, C11) Best known as the Paris base of Peter Brooks' experimental theatre troupe, this theatre also hosts works by other directors (notably Stéphane Lissner), as well as classical and jazz concerts.

✉ 37bis blvd de la Chapelle, 10e
☎ 01 46 07 34 50
Ⓜ La Chapelle
☺ Tues-Sat 8.30pm, Sat 4pm; box office Mon-Sat 11am-6pm **$** €11-20; matinees €8-17

Café de la Gare (5, C7)

One of the best and most innovative cafe-theatres in Paris, with acts ranging from reinterpreted classics to comic theatre and stand-up affairs.

✉ 41 rue du Temple, 4e ☎ 01 42 78 52 51
e www.cafe-de -la-gare.fr.st **Ⓜ** Hôtel de Ville, Rambuteau
☺ Wed-Sat 8 & 10pm
$ €16-19/8-16

Comédie Française

(3, D9) The world's oldest national theatre (founded in 1680 under Louis XIV), with a repertoire based on the works of French luminaries such as Corneille, Molière, Racine, Beaumarchais, Marivaux and Musset. In recent years contemporary and even non-French works have been staged in its three theatres.

✉ 2 rue de Richelieu, 1er ☎ 01 44 58 15 15
e www.comedie -francaise.fr **Ⓜ** Palais Royal ☺ box office 11am-6pm daily
$ €11-31; discounts for seniors & students

Laughing Matters

(3, B14) The best place in town for English-language belly laughs, hosting a regular stream of stand-ups from across the Channel, or drying out on the way back home from Edinburgh.

✉ Hôtel du Nord, 102 Quai de Jemmapes, 10e
☎ 01 48 06 01 20
e www.anythingmat ters.com
Ⓜ Jacques Bonsergent, République
☺ Sun-Tues 8.30pm
$ €19/16

Odéon Théâtre de l'Europe (5, B3)

This huge, ornate theatre, built in the early 1780s, stages great French classics as well as contemporary plays and works in their original languages (subtitled in French). It also often hosts theatre troupes from abroad.

✉ 1 Place Paul Claudel, 6e ☎ 01 44 41 36 36
e www.theatre-odeon .fr **Ⓜ** Odéon
☺ box office 11am-7pm **$** €5-28; discounted tickets available 90mins before curtain; discounts for seniors & students

Point Virgule (3, F13)

This popular spot in the Marais offers cafe-theatre at its best, with stand-up comics, performance artists, musical acts – you name it. The quality can be variable, but it's great fun nevertheless.

✉ 7 rue Ste-Croix de la Bretonnerie, 4e
☎ 01 42 78 67 03
Ⓜ Hôtel de Ville
☺ 8, 9.15 & 10.15pm
$ €14/20/23 for 1/2/3 shows, students €11 for 1 show (not Sat)

Théâtre de la Bastille

(2, F12) Probably the best fringe theatre venue in town, with a variety of experimental works including text, movement and music.

✉ 76 rue de la Roquette, 11e
☎ 01 43 57 42 14
e www.theatre-bastille.com
Ⓜ Bastille, Voltaire
☺ box office Mon-Fri 10am-1pm & 2-6.30pm, Sat-Sun 2-6.30pm
$ €19/28; discounts for seniors & students

CLASSICAL MUSIC, OPERA & DANCE

Centre Mandapa
(2, J10) Theatre dedicated to traditional and contemporary ethnic dance and theatre, with an emphasis on India (eg Kutiyattam dance theatre of Kerala).
✉ 6 rue Wurtz, 13e
☎ 01 45 89 01 60
Ⓜ Glacière Ⓢ €12-16/9-11

Cité de la Musique
(2, B13) The 1200-seat main auditorium hosts every imaginable type of music and dance. Students at the Conservatoire National Supérieur de Musique Musique et de la Danse (☎ 01 40 40 45 45) perform free orchestral concerts and recitals several times a week.
✉ 221 av Jean Jaurès, 19e ☎ 01 44 84 45 45
ⓔ www.cite-musique .fr Ⓜ Porte de Pantin
🕐 box office Tues-Sun noon-6pm Ⓢ €12-30; discounts for seniors & students

Opéra Bastille
(3, G15) The Opéra National de Paris splits its performances between here and the Opéra Garnier, its old home. The Opéra Bastille opened in 1989 and, like the Opéra Garnier, also stages ballets and concerts put on by the Opéra National's affiliated orchestra, choir and ballet companies. The opera season lasts from mid-September to mid-July.
✉ 2-6 Place de la Bastille, 12e
☎ 08 92 69 78 68
ⓔ www.opera-de-paris .fr Ⓜ Bastille 🕐 box office Mon-Sat 11am-6.30pm Ⓢ €10-105 opera, €8-64 ballet, €7-39 concerts; 15mins before curtain unsold tickets are €16 for students, youths & seniors; book online, or by mail (Opéra National de Paris, 120 rue de Lyon, 75576 Paris Cedex 12) 10wks ahead, or by phone 4wks ahead

Opéra Comique
(3, B10) A century-old hall that plays host to classic and lesser-known works of opera. The season lasts from late October to early July.
✉ 5 rue Favart, 2e
☎ 08 25 00 00 58
ⓔ www.opera-comique .com Ⓜ Richelieu Drouot 🕐 box office (opp 14 rue Favart) Mon-Sat 9am-9pm, Sun 11am-7pm Ⓢ €7-170; €8 tickets with limited visibility up to 12hrs before curtain; discounts 15mins before curtain for students, youth & seniors

---

Bookings & Tickets
Reservations are recommended for all performances. You can buy tickets for many (but not all) cultural events at several ticket outlets, among them **FNAC** (☎ 08 03 02 00 40 or ☎ 08 92 68 36 22 for reservations in French) outlets and **Virgin Megastore** (☎ 01 49 53 50 00), 52 av des Champs Élysées, 8e (3, C4). Both make reservations and do ticketing by phone.

Kiosque Théâtre sells half-price tickets (plus €2.45 commission) for same-day performances. The two agencies, in front of Gare Montparnasse, 15e (3, K7), and opposite 15 Place de la Madeleine, 9e (3, C7), are open Tues-Sat 12.30-8pm, Sun 12.30-4pm.

Opéra Bastille

Rob Flynn

Chagall's gloriously ornate ceiling, Opéra Garnier (p. 39)

Simon Bracken

Opéra Garnier (3, B9)
The extravagant Opéra Garnier is the traditional home of the Opéra National de Paris (see also Opéra Bastille above). While most of the major opera performances are held at Bastille, the Opéra Garnier offers outstanding acoustics, though not all seats have great views.
☒ **Place de l'Opéra, 9e**
☎ **08 92 69 78 68**
ⓔ **www.opera-de-paris .fr** Ⓜ **Opéra** ⊙ **box office Mon-Sat 11am-6.30pm** Ⓢ **€7-105 opera, €7-64 ballet; 15mins before curtain unsold tickets €15 for** students, youth & seniors; tickets on sale 2wks prior to performances; booking details as per Opéra Bastille

Regard du Cygne
(2, D13) Many of Paris' young and daring talents in movement, music and theatre congregate around this interesting performance space in Belleville. If you're in the mood for some innovative modern dance – performance or participation – this is the place.
☒ **210 rue de Belleville, 20e** ☎ **01 43 58 55 93**
Ⓜ **Place des Fêtes**
Ⓢ **€8/5;** discounts for students, seniors & unemployed 30mins before curtain

Salle Pleyel (3, A3)
A highly regarded, 1920s-era hall that hosts many of Paris' finest classical music concerts and recitals.
☒ **252 rue du Faubourg St-Honoré, 8e**
☎ **01 45 61 53 00**
ⓔ **www.salle-pleyel.fr**
Ⓜ **Ternes** ⊙ **box office Mon-Sat 11am-6pm**
Ⓢ **€13-62**

Théâtre des Champs Élysées (3, D4)
A prestigious Right Bank orchestral and recital hall, infamous as the venue where Stravinsky debuted his controversial *Le Sacre du Printemps* in 1913. Popular Sunday concerts are held year-round at 11am.
☒ **15 ave Montaigne, 8e** ☎ **01 49 52 50 50**
ⓔ **www.theatre champselysees.fr**
Ⓜ **Alma-Marceau**
⊙ **box office Mon-Sat 1-7pm** Ⓢ **€8-110**

Théâtre Musical de Paris (5, B6)
Also called the Théâtre Municipal du Châtelet or just the Théâtre du Châtelet, this hall hosts operas, concerts (including some by the excellent Orchestre de Paris) and theatre performances.
☒ **1 Place du Châtelet, 1er** ☎ **01 42 33 00 00; reservations 01 40 28 28 40** ⓔ **www .chatelet-theatre.com**
Ⓜ **Châtelet**
⊙ **box office Mon-Sat 11am-7pm**
Ⓢ **€8-110 opera, €14-30 ballet, Sun concerts €3.05/1.50**

ROCK, JAZZ & FRENCH CHANSONS

There's rock at numerous bars, cafes and clubs around. Typically, tickets cost €18-40. The most popular stadium venues for international acts include **Le Zénith** (☎ 01 42 08 60 00) at the **Cité de la Musique** (p. 29), and the **Palais Omnisports de Paris-Bercy** (☎ 08 03 03 00 31; p. 100).

Le Baiser Salé (5, B6)
The Salty Kiss is one of three very hip jazz clubs on the same street. The *salle de jazz* on the 1st floor has concerts of Afro jazz, jazz fusion etc. There's a bar on the ground floor.
✉ **58 rue des Lombards, 1er** ☎ **01 42 33 37 71**
Ⓜ **Châtelet**
◷ bar 7pm-6am; salle de jazz 10pm-3am
Ⓢ €7-16; Sun-Mon free

Le Bataclan (5, C10)
Popular mid-sized venue featuring an eclectic mix of international rock, French bands, world music and even French *chanson*.
✉ **50 blvd Voltaire, 11e**
☎ **01 43 14 35 35**
Ⓜ **Oberkampf**
◷ 8pm-late Ⓢ €16-32

Le Caveau de la Huchette (5, C4)
A medieval *caveau* (cellar) – used as a torture chamber during the Revolution – where virtually all the jazz greats have played since 1946. It's touristy, but the atmosphere can often be more electric than at the more 'serious' jazz clubs. Details on coming attractions are posted on the door.
✉ **5 rue de la Huchette, 5e** ☎ **01 43 26 65 05**
Ⓜ **St-Michel** ◷ 9.30pm-2.30am (Fri 3.30am, Sat 4am) Ⓢ **Mon-Thurs €10; Fri-Sat €11**

Chez Louisette (2, A9)
This is one of the highlights of a visit to Paris' largest flea market. Market-goers crowd around little tables to eat lunch and hear an old-time chanteuse belt out Edith Piaf numbers accompanied by accordion music.
✉ **Marché aux Puces de St-Ouen, inside the maze of Marché Vernaison near 130 av Michelet**
☎ **01 40 12 10 14**
Ⓜ **Porte de Clignancourt**
◷ Sat-Mon noon-7pm

La Cigale (4, E6)
This converted theatre has been a favourite of visiting rock, punk and indie bands for years. It's also a fave of audiences with its huge capacity, faded good looks and bouncy mosh pit.
✉ **102 blvd Rochechouart, 18e**
☎ **01 49 25 89 99**
Ⓜ **Pigalle** ◷ 8.30pm
Ⓢ **variable**

You don't need the agility of a rabbit to have a hopping good time.

Simon Bracken

Le Divan du Monde
(4, E5) One of the best concert venues in town with good visibility and sound; Latino figures at least once a week. It's also a popular club, open most nights till dawn.
✉ 75 rue des Martyrs
☎ 01 44 92 77 66
Ⓜ Pigalle ⌚ Mon-Sat from 7.30pm, Sun from 2pm ⑤ Tues-Sun €10-20, Mon free

Au Duc des Lombards
(5, B6) This ultra-cool venue, decorated with posters of past jazz greats, attracts a far more relaxed (and less reverent) crowd than the other two venues on the same street.
✉ 42 rue des Lombards, 1er ☎ 01 42 33 22 88
Ⓜ Châtelet
⌚ 8pm-4am ⑤ €13-19

Le Lapin Agile (4, B5)
A rustic cabaret venue favoured by turn-of-the-century artists and intellectuals. The name derives from Le Lapin à Gill, a mural of a rabbit jumping out of a cooking pot by caricaturist André Gill, which can still be seen on the western exterior wall. These days, chansons are performed and poetry read nightly.
✉ 22 rue des Saules, 18e ☎ 01 46 06 85 87
Ⓜ Lamarck Caulaincourt
⌚ Tues-Sun 9pm-2am
⑤ €20/14

Théâtre du Tourtour
(5, B7) This is an intimate, 123-seat theatre housed in a 15th-century cellar. The entertainment includes plays by young theatre companies at 7pm; classical or modern plays by more experienced actors at 8.30pm; music – anything from rock to French chansons – at 10.15pm.
✉ 20 rue Quincampoix, 4e ☎ 01 48 87 82 48
Ⓜ Châtelet ⌚ Tues-Sat 10pm ⑤ €11-16

Au Vieux Paris (5, C7)
A real period-piece Parisian bar which hosts sing-alongs of French chansons (sheet music provided), accompanied by an accordionist and Madame Françoise, the feisty proprietor. The patrons are mostly young Parisians. Arrive around 11pm to get a seat.
✉ 72 rue de la Verrerie, 4e ☎ 01 48 87 55 56
Ⓜ Hôtel de Ville
⌚ Thurs-Sat 11.45pm

La Villa (3, F9)
This very cool, high-tech place attracts big-name performers from around the world, with local talent thrown in for good measure between sets. You'll love the unusual furnishings – stools shaped like teardrops, 'crouching' chairs etc.
✉ 29 rue Jacob, 6e
☎ 01 43 26 60 00
Ⓜ St-Germain des Prés
⌚ Mon-Sat 10.30pm-2am ⑤ €18-23

DANCE CLUBS

Les Bains Douches
(3, D12) Cooler-than-thou glam celebrity hangout, but with a very satisfying garage/house mix. Wear your best party outfit and don't take non for an answer.
✉ 7 rue du Bourg-l'Abbé, 3e
☎ 01 48 87 01 80
Ⓜ Étienne Marcel
⌚ 11.30pm-5am
⑤ €16-20

Le Balajo (2, F12)
A mainstay of the Parisian dance-hall scene since 1936. Wednesday is mambo night; Thursday, salsa; Friday and Saturday the DJs spin rock, 1970s disco, funk etc. On Sunday afternoon, DJs play old-fashioned musette (accordion music) – waltz, tango, cha-cha – for aficionados of rétro tea dancing. Jacket required.
✉ 9 rue de Lappe, 11e
☎ 01 47 00 07 87
Ⓜ Bastille ⌚ Mon-Sat 11.30pm-5.30am, Sun 3-7pm ⑤ €8-16

Batofar (2, H12)
One of the coolest venues in town, the Batofar is an Irish lighthouse-boat, moored on the Seine, with a bar/restaurant on top and club inside. The club has a diverse music policy – electrodub, techno, deep house, reggae – and aims to push the boundaries.
✉ opp. 11 Quai François Mauriac, 13e
☎ 01 56 29 10 00
ⓔ www.batofar.org
Ⓜ Bibliothèque François Mitterand, Quai de la Gare

La Chapelle des Lombards (2, F12)
Something of a pick-up place, where Antillean, African and Latin American beats create a very lively

salsa scene. There's usually a live concert Thursday. Punters wearing trainers (sneakers) won't get in.
✉ **19 rue de Lappe, 11e** ☎ **01 43 57 24 24**
Ⓜ **Bastille**
🕓 **Tues-Fri 10.30pm-5am (to 6pm Sat-Sun)**
⑤ **€16-20; free for women before midnight**

Le Gibus (3, C15)

This former rock mecca (Police, the Clash) is now a techno venue and still attracts a somewhat dodgy clientele. Free trance parties Wednesdays.
✉ **18 rue du Faubourg-du-Temple, 11e**
☎ **01 47 00 78 88**
Ⓜ **République**
🕓 **Tues 9pm-dawn, Wed-Sun midnight-dawn**
⑤ **€7-15, Wed-Thurs free**

Batofar by day

Rob Flynn

Boîtes

A *boîte* (literally 'box') is just about any club where music leads to dancing. The truly *branché* (trendy) crowd considers showing up before 1am a serious breach of good taste.

The *boîtes* favoured by the Parisian 'in' crowd change frequently, and many are officially private. Single men may not be admitted, even if their clothes are subculturally appropriate. Women, on the other hand, get in for free on some nights. It's always easier to get into the club of your choice during the week – when things may be hopping even more than they are at the weekend. Parisians tend to go out in groups and may not mingle as much as you're used to.

La Java (2, D12)

The original dance hall where Piaf got her first break now reverberates to the sound of salsa at the Cuban jam sessions, featuring live and recorded sounds and some hot dancing.
✉ **105 rue du Faubourg-du-Temple, 10e** ☎ **01 42 02 20 52**
Ⓜ **Belleville** 🕓 **Thurs-Fri 11pm-6am** ⑤ **€9-16**

La Locomotive (4, D3)

A huge, ever-popular disco that's long been one of the favourite dancing venues for teenage out-of-towners. Music ranges from techno in the pulsating basement to groove and disco in the 1st-floor loft; psychedelic, rock and the like dominate on the huge ground floor. There's a popular gay tea dance here on Sunday from 5-11pm.
✉ **90 blvd de Clichy, 18e** ☎ **01 53 41 88 88**
Ⓜ **Blanche**
🕓 **11pm-6am (Sat-Sun to 7am, Mon from midnight)** ⑤ **€9-16**

Rex Club (3, C11)

Laurent Garnier made his name at this huge, popular techno and house club, which features music and video DJs. Name DJs play here regularly.
✉ **5 blvd Poissonière, 2e** ☎ **01 42 36 83 98**
Ⓜ **Bonne Nouvelle**
🕓 **Tues-Sat 11pm-dawn**
⑤ **€9-16**

Slow Club (5, A6)

An unpretentious club housed in a deep cellar once used to ripen Caribbean bananas. The live bands attract students as well as older couples. The music varies from night to night but includes jazz, boogie, bebop, swing and blues.
✉ **130 rue de Rivoli, 1er** ☎ **01 42 33 84 30**
Ⓜ **Châtelet** 🕓 **Tues-Sat 10pm-3am (Fri-Sat to 4am)** ⑤ **€9-13**

Zed Club (5, C4)

An arched stone basement where the DJs favour rock 'n' roll, jazz and swing.
✉ **2 rue des Anglais, 5e** ☎ **01 43 54 93 78**
Ⓜ **Maubert-Mutualité**
🕓 **Wed-Sat 10.30pm-3am (to 5am Fri-Sat)**
⑤ **€9-16**

CINEMAS

Pariscope (**e** www.pariscope.com) and *L'Officiel des Spectacles* list the cinematic offerings alphabetically by their French title followed by the English (or German, Italian, Spanish etc) one. If a movie is labelled 'vo' (for *version originale*) it means it will be subtitled rather than dubbed ('vf' or *version française*), so 'vo' Hollywood movies will still be in English.

Le Champo (5, C3)
One of the most popular of the many Quartier Latin cinemas, featuring classics and retrospectives along the lines of Hitchcock, Jacques Tati, Frank Capra and Woody Allen.
☒ 51 rue des Écoles, 5e ☎ 01 43 54 51 60
Ⓜ St-Michel, Cluny-La Sorbonne ⑤ €7/6; matinee €4.50

Cinéma des Cinéastes
(4, D1) Founded by the three Claudes (Miller, Berri and Lelouch) and *Betty Blue* director Jean-Jacques Beneix, this three-screen cinema is dedicated to quality cinema, whether French, foreign or avant-garde. Thematic seasons, documentaries and meet-the-director sessions round out the program.
☒ 7 av de Clichy, 17e ☎ 01 53 42 40 20
Ⓜ Place de Clichy ⑤ €7/5.50

Cinémathèque Française (3, D2)
This government-supported cultural institution almost always leaves its foreign offerings – often seldom-screened classics – in the original, nondubbed version. There are two cinemas, one at the Palais de Chaillot, the other at 42 blvd Bonne Nouvelle, 10e (3, C12).
☒ Palais de Chaillot, 7 av Albert de Mun, 16e

☎ 01 56 26 01 01
ℯ www.cinema thequefrancaise.com
Ⓜ Trocadéro, Iéna
⧖ Tues-Sun
⑤ €4.50/3

Grand Action (5, E4)
The flagship cinema of the Action chain, which specialises in grand cinema events in both English and French – often new prints of classics such as Kubrick's *Spartacus*. Retrospectives include gems from the Golden Years of Hollywood or more recent classics such as the films of Jim Jarmusch.
☒ 5 rue des Écoles, 5e ☎ 01 43 29 44 40
Ⓜ Cardinal Lemoine ⑤ €6/4

Le Studio des Ursulines (3, J10)
Legendary art-house cinema nowadays adopting a more

eclectic program of first-release avant-garde pieces, retrospectives, lost classics and more popular movies.
☒ 10 rue des Ursulines, 5e ☎ 01 43 26 19 09
Ⓜ Châtelet-Les Halles
ℛ RER Luxembourg
⑤ €6/5

UGC CinéCité Les Halles (3, E11)
The enormous 16-screen cinema complex in the underground Les Halles shopping centre screens mainly first-run features, including Hollywood blockbusters. The seats are among the most comfortable in town, and some of the screens are so wide you need to turn your head tennis-match style to follow an onscreen conversation.
☒ Forum des Halles, 1er ☎ 08 36 68 68 58
Ⓜ Châtelet-Les Halles ⑤ €8

Going to the Movies
Going to the movies in Paris does not come cheaply: expect to pay around €8 for a ticket. Students and people under 18 and over 60 usually get discounts of about 25% except on Fri, Sat and Sun nights. On Wed (and sometimes Mon) most cinemas give discounts to everyone.

Rob Flynn

PUBS, BARS & CAFES

L'Apparement Café
(5, D8) Not a single lapse of taste mars the studied untidiness of this home away from home, tucked behind the Musée Picasso. Wood panelling, leather sofas, parlour games and dog-eared books add to its charm.
✉ 18 rue des Coutures St-Germain, 3e
☎ 01 48 87 12 22
Ⓜ Filles du Calvaire
🕒 Mon-Fri noon-2am, Sat 4pm-2am, Sun 12.30pm-midnight

L'Armagnac (2, F13)
A bustling lunch spot by day, by night the Armagnac has just the right levels of smoke, noise and local flavour to give it the authenticity that more self-conscious bars closer to Bastille struggle to replicate.
✉ 104 rue de Charonne, 11e ☎ 01 43 71 49 43
Ⓜ Charonne
🕒 Mon-Fri 7am-2am, Sat-Sun 10.30am-2am

L'Autre Café (2, E12)
With its long bar, open spaces, relaxed environment and reasonable prices this cafe attracts a mixed young crowd of locals, artists and party-goers.
✉ 62 rue Jean-Pierre Timbaud, 11e
☎ 01 40 21 03 07
Ⓜ Parmentier
🕒 9am-1.30am

Buddha Bar (3, C7)
At centre stage in the cavernous cellar of this restaurant/bar frequented by suits, supermodels and hangers-in is an enormous bronze Buddha. Everyone should go at least once for a look, but stick with the

Fill 'er up.

drinks (cocktails from €10); a Pacific Rim-style meal will cost you upwards of €45.
✉ 8 rue Boissy d'Anglas, 8e ☎ 01 53 05 90 00 Ⓜ Concorde
🕒 6pm-2am

Café Noir (3, C11)
It may be a bit out of the way, being on the edge of the Sentier garments district, but this funky cafe/bar draws a crowd of Anglo and Francophones well into the night, attracted by the friendly ambience and reasonable prices.
✉ 65 rue Montmartre, 2e ☎ 01 40 39 07 36
Ⓜ Sentier 🕒 Mon-Fri 8am-2am, Sat 4pm-2am

Café Oz (5, D3)
A casual, friendly Australian pub with Foster's on tap, plus Australian wines by the glass. The Aussie staff are clued in about jobs, apartments etc. There's a second Café Oz across the river at 18 rue Saint Denis, 1er (5, B6), and a third at 1 rue de Bruxelles, 9e (4, D3), opposite Moulin Rouge.
✉ 184 rue St-Jacques, 5e ☎ 01 43 54 30 48
🚇 RER Luxembourg
🕒 4pm-2am (happy hour to 9.30pm)

China Club (2, G12)
This stylish establishment has a restaurant and huge bar with high ceilings on the ground floor, a *fumoir* on the 1st floor and a jazz club in the cellar – all done up to look like Shanghai circa 1930. Happy hour is 7-9pm daily when all drinks (including the excellent martinis) are €5.35.
✉ 50 rue de Charenton, 12e ☎ 01 43 43 82 02
Ⓜ Ledru Rollin
🕒 7pm-2am

La Closerie des Lilas
(3, K9) Anyone who's ever read Hemingway knows he did a lot of writing, drinking and eating of oysters at this classy bar, and little brass tags on the tables tell you exactly where he (and other luminaries such as Picasso, Apollinaire etc) whiled away the hours being creative or just gossiping. Great summer terrace.
✉ 171 blvd du Montparnasse, 6e
☎ 01 40 51 34 50
🚇 RER Port Royal
🕒 11.30am-1am

Le Clown Bar (5, D10)
This wonderful wine bar next to the Cirque d'Hiver is like a museum with painted ceilings, mosaics and a lovely round bar. The food is simple and unpretentious.
✉ **114 rue Amelot, 11e**
☎ **01 43 55 87 35**
Ⓜ **Filles du Calvaire**
🕐 **Mon-Sat noon-3pm & 7.30pm-1am, Sun 7pm-1am**

Comptoir Paris-Marrakech (3, E10)
A languid little terrace near frantic Les Halles. During the day you can sip herbal tea or cinnamon milk, or down a *pastis* with liquorice as the sun sets on St Eustache.
✉ **37 rue Berger, 1er**
☎ **01 40 26 26 66**
Ⓜ **Châtelet-Les Halles**
🕐 **noon-2am (to 3am Fri & Sat)**

Les Étages (5, C7)
Head upstairs to the two upper floors for grunge, with graffiti on the walls and big leather armchairs. The drinks aren't cheap (€10 for spirits), but you do get to phone through your order on an ancient 1950s telephone. Happy hour is 5-9pm.
✉ **35 rue Vieille du Temple, 4e**
☎ **01 42 72 81 34**
Ⓜ **Hôtel de Ville**
🕐 **11am-2am**

La Flèche d'Or Café (2, F14) This bar – in a disused train station southeast of Père Lachaise Cemetery – attracts a trendy and arty (not to forget grungy) young crowd, with some great vibes; this may as well be Berlin. The big cafe here does a decent brunch on Sunday.
✉ **102bis rue de Bagnolet, 20e** ☎ **01 43 72 04 23** Ⓜ **Porte de Bagnolet** 🕐 **10am-2am**

Le Fumoir (3, E10)
This huge bar/cafe across the road from the Louvre has a gentleman's club/library theme and is run by the proprietors of the China Club. It's friendly, buzzy and good fun.
✉ **6 rue de l'Amiral Coligny, 1er**
☎ **01 42 92 00 24**
Ⓜ **Louvre-Rivoli**
🕐 **11am-2am; food noon-3pm & 7-11pm**

Harry's Bar (3, C9)
One of the most popular prewar American bars (*habitués* included Hemingway and Scott Fitzgerald), this place still makes the best martini in Paris. The Cuban mahogany bar was imported from Manhattan's 3rd Ave in 1911.
✉ **5 rue Daunou, 2e**
☎ **01 42 61 71 14**
Ⓜ **Opéra** 🕐 **Mon-Sat 10.30am-4am**

Waiting for that train that never comes at la Flèche d'Or Café.

Simon Bracken

Le Mecano Bar (2, E12)
Housed in a former tool shed, the ultra-cool Mecano is a good place to meet before heading elsewhere around rue Oberkampf to eat and party.
✉ **99 rue Oberkampf, 11e ☎ 01 40 21 35 28 Ⓜ Parmentier**
🕐 **8pm-2am**

La Perla (5, D7)
A favourite with younger Parisians, this trendy California-style Mexican bar serves up guacamole, nachos and burritos. Happy hour (cocktails, tequila and mezcal only) is weekdays only, 6-8pm.
✉ **26 rue François Miron, 4e ☎ 01 42 77 59 40 Ⓜ Hôtel de Ville, St-Paul 🕐 Mon-Fri noon-3pm & 7-11pm, Sat-Sun noon-11pm**

Le Petit Fer à Cheval (3, F13) A slightly offbeat bar/restaurant named after its horseshoe-shaped counter, this place is often filled to overflowing with friendly, mostly straight young regulars. The *plat du jour* changes each day. The all stainless-steel bathroom is straight out of a Flash Gordon film.
✉ **30 rue Vieille du Temple, 4e ☎ 01 42 72 47 47 Ⓜ Hôtel de Ville, St-Paul 🕐 9am-2am (weekends from 11am); food noon-1.15am**

Le Pick Clops (5, D7)
In a very gay neighbourhood, this straight, downmarket rock bar with cheap drinks is a great place to watch the world go by. The brief happy hour is 8-9pm.
✉ **16 rue Vieille du Temple, 4e**
☎ **01 40 29 02 18**

Apéritifs

Early evening is *apéritif* time in cafes throughout Paris. The most popular tipples are wine (*rouge* or *blanc*); beer (*une pression* is a draught beer); *pastis*, an aniseed-flavoured drink mixed with water to taste; and *kir*, an extract of blackberries normally mixed with white wine, or with champagne to make a *kir royal*.

Ⓜ **Hôtel de Ville**
🕐 **Mon-Sat 8am-2am, Sun 2pm-midnight**

Piment Café (5, D8)
This small and cosmopolitan bar changes face frequently, with tranquil moments punctuated by live music, art on show and good, reasonably priced food.
✉ **15 rue de Sévigné, 4e ☎ 01 42 74 33 75 Ⓜ St-Paul 🕐 noon-1am (Sun from 6pm)**

SanzSans (2, F12)
By night this full-on watering hole is one of the liveliest (OK, rowdiest) drinking spots on the Bastille beat: dress (or undress) to impress. By day the Baroque decor seems a mite overdone.
✉ **49 rue du Faubourg St-Antoine, 11e**
☎ **01 44 75 78 78**
Ⓜ **Bastille 🕐 9am-2am**

Le Troisième Bureau (3, D15) A pub-cum-*bistrot* with an interesting clientele where you can read, listen to music and even send or receive a fax.
✉ **74 rue de la Folie**

Méricourt, 11e
☎ **01 43 55 87 65**
Ⓜ **Oberkampf**
🕐 **11.30am-2am (Sun from 6.30pm)**

Le Viaduc Café (2, G12)
The terrace of this very trendy cafe in one of the glassed-in arches of the Viaduc des Arts is an excellent spot to while away the hours, and the jazz brunch on Sunday is very popular.
✉ **43 ave Daumesnil, 12e ☎ 01 44 74 70 70 Ⓜ Gare de Lyon**
🕐 **9am-4am**

Le Violon Dingue (5, D4) A loud, lively and none-too-spotless American-style bar that attracts lots of English speakers in their early 20s. American sporting events like the Superbowl (football) and the NBA (basketball) play-offs are shown on the large-screen TV.
✉ **46 rue de la Montagne Ste-Geneviève, 5e**
☎ **01 43 25 79 93**
Ⓜ **Maubert-Mutualité**
🕐 **6pm-1.30am; happy hour 6-10pm**

GAY & LESBIAN PARIS

The Marais – especially the areas around the intersection of rue des Archives and rue Ste-Croix de la Bretonnerie (4e), and eastward to rue Vieille du Temple – has been Paris' main centre of gay social life since the early 1980s. There are also some decent bars west of blvd de Sébastopol in the 1er and 2e.

L'Arène (5, C6)
For those seriously OFB (out for business), this place can oblige. It's got dark rooms and cubicles on three levels and heats up (boils over, rather) from around midnight. Take the usual precautions.
✉ **80 Quai de l'Hôtel de Ville, 4e**
Ⓜ **Hôtel de Ville**
🕐 **2pm-6am (to 7am Sat-Sun)**

Parisians aren't known for being straight-laced.

Banana Café (5, B6)
This ever-popular male cruise bar on two levels has an enclosed terrace with stand-up tables and attracts a young, buffed crowd.
✉ **13 rue de la Ferronnerie, 1er**
☎ **01 42 33 35 31**
Ⓜ **Châtelet-Les Halles**
🕐 **4pm-6am; happy hour 4.30-7.30pm**

La Champmesle (3, C9)
A relaxed, dimly lit place that plays mellow music for its patrons, about 75% of whom are lesbians (the rest are mostly gay men). The back room is reserved for women only. Traditional French *chansons* are performed live every Thursday at 10pm.
✉ **4 rue Chabanais, 2e**
☎ **01 42 96 85 20**
Ⓜ **Pyramides**
🕐 **Mon-Sat 5pm-5am**

Le Cox (5, C7)
OK, it's got an in-your-face name but this small bar attracts an interesting (and interested) crowd throughout the evening.
✉ **15 rue des Archives, 4e** ☎ **01 42 72 08 00**
Ⓜ **Hôtel de Ville**
🕐 **1pm-2am; happy hour 6-9pm**

Duplex Bar (5, B8)
One of the oldest gay bars in Paris (in every sense), the dark, avant-garde Duplex doubles as something of a gallery with art shows every month.
✉ **25 rue Michel Le**

Comte, 3e
☎ **01 42 72 80 86**
Ⓜ **Rambuteau**
🕐 **8pm-2am**

Open Café (5, C7)
This is the place people head for after work to start off the evening. It gets so packed that the clientele spills out onto the pavement.
✉ **17 rue des Archives, 4e** ☎ **01 42 72 26 18**
Ⓜ **Hôtel de Ville**
🕐 **10am-2am; happy hour 6-8pm**

Le Queen (3, B4)
The best spot in town for all-night drag party action. 'Boys Only' Thursday and 'Disco Inferno' Monday.
✉ **102 av des Champs Élysées, 8e** ☎ **01 53 89 08 90** Ⓜ **George V**
🕐 **11pm-dawn** 💲 **free Mon-Fri; Sat-Sun €16**

Quetzal Bar (5, C7)
A neon-lit, ultramodern bar popular with gay 30-something men – cruisy and attitude free.
✉ **10 rue de la Verrerie, 4e** ☎ **01 48 87 99 07**
Ⓜ **Hôtel de Ville**
🕐 **5pm-3am (to 4am Fri-Sat); happy hours 5-8pm & 11pm-midnight**

Les Scandaleuses
(5, D7) Glossy and lively lesbian bar in the Marais, popular with artists and designers. Women only.
✉ **8 rue des Écouffes, 4e**
☎ **01 48 87 39 26**
Ⓜ **Hôtel de Ville**
🕐 **6pm-2am**

SPECTATOR SPORTS

For details on upcoming sporting events, consult the sports daily *L'Équipe*, or *Figaroscope* published by *Le Figaro* each Wednesday.

Since 1974 the final stage of the Tour de France, the world's most prestigious **cycling** event, has concluded on the Champs Élysées. The final day varies from year to year but is usually the afternoon of the 3rd or 4th Sunday in July. The frenetic pace of track cycling comes to the Palais Omnisports de Paris-Bercy (see below) in winter with the Grand Prix des Nations (October) and the Paris Six-Day (January).

Le foot (**soccer**) has gained even more popularity since France won the World Cup at home in 1998, and Paris hosts its fair share of international events. Paris-Saint Germain football team plays its home games at the Parc des Princes. The 80,000-seat Stade de France in Saint Denis hosted the World Cup finals, and is the major venue for soccer and rugby alike.

If fillies are your thing, there are six racecourses around Paris for you to lose your shirt. One of the cheapest ways to spend a relaxing afternoon in the company of Parisians from all walks of life is to go to the **races**. The Hippodrome d'Auteuil (2, F3) is the most accessible of Paris' racecourses, and hosts steeplechases from February to early July and early September to early December. The minimum bet is only €2. *Paris Turf* publishes a program.

Show jumping is all the rage in Paris and the Jumping International de Paris, held in March at the Palais Omnisports de Paris-Bercy, attracts thousands of fans.

Rugby is a popular sport in France and the local club is Le Racing Club de France, whose home ground is Stade Yves du Manoir in Colombe.

In late May/early June the world of **tennis** focuses on the clay surface of Stade Roland Garros in the Bois de Boulogne for the second of the four Grand Slam tournaments. The Paris Indoor tournament is held in late October/early November at the Palais Omnisports de Paris-Bercy.

Sports Venues

Paris is not a great sporting city, but it does have a few decent venues for major and international events.

Palais Omnisports de Paris-Bercy (2, H12) blvd de Bercy, 12e ☎ 01 44 68 44 68 **e** www.bercy.fr **M** Bercy **🚌** 20, 24, 63, 87

Stade de France (1, B7) rue Francis de Pressensé, Saint Denis ☎ 01 55 93 00 00 **e** www.stadedefrance.fr **🚆** RER line B or D to Stade de France

Parc des Princes (2, G2) 24 rue du Commandant-Guilbaud, 16e ☎ 01 42 30 03 60 **e** www.psg.fr **M** Porte d'Auteuil

Stade Roland-Garros (2, G2) 2 av Gordon Bennett, 16e ☎ 01 47 43 48 00 **e** www.frenchopen.org **M** Porte d'Auteuil **🚌** 22, 32, 52, 62, 72

Palais Omnisports de Paris-Bercy

Rob Flynn

places to stay

There's a huge variety of accommodation in Paris, ranging from sumptuous palaces and converted 17th-century townhouses to poky little holes where you wouldn't tether your dog. And while there's something like 1500 hotels in the city, nearly 20 million visitors a year gobble up the available rooms pretty quickly. The most interesting hotels can be booked out weeks, if not months, in advance: high season is May-October, and in January and March many upmarket hotels can be busy for the fashion shows; at other times, Paris' burgeoning trade fair business can also make accommodation tight in an otherwise normal week. On the other

Room Rates

The price ranges in this chapter indicate the cost per night of a standard double room. Seasonal variations can apply.

Deluxe	€200-600
Top End	€75-199
Mid-Range	€55-74
Budget	€15-54

hand, in July and particularly August, when businesses close for the summer, many hotels drop their rates to attract tourists. The best advice: book as far ahead as you can.

Bookings

If you get stuck, the Paris tourist office at 127 av des Champs Élysées, 8e (3, B3; ☎ 08 36 68 31 12; Ⓜ George V; 9am-8pm)) or at Gare de Lyon (2, G12; Ⓜ Gare de Lyon), can find you a place to stay for the night for a small fee.

Often (but not always) room rates will include breakfast – usually croissants and rolls plus tea and coffee. Make it clear on arrival whether or not you want breakfast at the hotel; most people opt for breakfast on a cafe terrace rather than in a dingy dining room.

Hotels expect you to check in by 6pm. It's a good idea in this busiest of tourist cities to ring if you are going to arrive any later to assure your reservation is retained. Checkout is noon.

Staying in Paris is all charm until you hit those stairs with your luggage.

DELUXE

L'Hôtel (3, F9)
Tucked away in a quiet quay-side street, L'Hôtel is the stuff of romantic Paris legends and proudly carries its name as *the* hotel. Rock and film star patrons alike fight to sleep in the room where Oscar Wilde slept his last a century ago or in the mirrored Art Deco room of legendary dancer Mistinguett.
✉ **13 rue des Beaux Arts, 6e** ☎ **01 44 41 99 00; fax 01 43 25 64 81**
e **www.l-hotel.com**
Ⓜ **St-Germain des Prés**
✕ **restaurant**

Hôtel Costes (3, C8)
Jean-Louis Costes' eponymous four-star hotel, opened in 1995, offers a luxurious and immoderate home away from home, in the heart of one of the city's chicest shopping quarters.
✉ **239 rue St-Honoré, 1er** ☎ **01 42 44 50 00; fax 01 44 44 50 01**
e **www.hotel-costes .com** Ⓜ **Concorde**
✕ **restaurant**

Hôtel de Lutèce (5, E6)
This exquisite little hotel, more country than city, is in the heart of one of Paris' most charming quarters. The comfortable rooms are tastefully decorated, the staff are friendly and the location is probably the most desirable in all France.
✉ **65 rue St-Louis en l'Île, 4e** ☎ **01 43 26 23 52; fax 01 43 29 60 25**
Ⓜ **Pont Marie**

Hôtel Raphaël (3, B2)
Discretion is the watch-word of this richly (and authentically) furnished *petit palace* (with 90 rooms, including 38 apartments), just a quick limo ride from the Champs Élysées. The view from the 7th-floor terrace restaurant is one of the finest in all of Paris. And the mock-Gothic bar offers welcome sanctuary from those pesky paparazzi.
✉ **17 av Kléber, 16e** ☎ **01 53 64 32 00; fax 01 53 64 32 01**
e **www.raphael-hotel .com** Ⓜ **Kléber**
✕ **La Salle à Manger**

Hôtel Ritz (3, C8)
Irving Berlin may have had Park Ave in mind, but this is *the* place for puttin' it on. Owned by Mohamed Al Fayed (Dodi's father and Harrod's owner) the Ritz has class and swank throughout from the €1400-a-night Coco Chanel apartments to the Hemingway Bar and the Espadon restaurant (two Michelin stars).
✉ **15 Place Vendôme, 1er** ☎ **01 43 16 30 70; fax 01 43 16 31 78**
e **www.ritzparis.com**
Ⓜ **Opéra** ✕ **Espadon, Ritz Club, Vendôme Bar, Hemingway Bar**

While you are putting on the Ritz you had may as well roll out the red carpet.

Simon Bracken

TOP END

Hôtel d'Angleterre

(3, F9) A beautiful and very popular hotel in a quiet street close to busy blvd St-Germain and the Musée d'Orsay. The loyal clientele breakfast or brunch in the courtyard garden of this former British Embassy where Hemingway once lodged (Room 14).

✉ 44 rue Jacob, 6e
☎ 01 42 60 34 72;
fax 01 42 60 16 93
ℯ anglhotel
@wanadoo.fr
Ⓜ St-Germain des Prés

Comfort for the entire clan.

Hôtel Brighton (3, D8)

The recently renovated Brighton has wonderful views over the Jardin des Tuileries (and, from the 4th and 5th floors, over the trees to the Seine), and is handy to just about everything.

✉ 218 rue de Rivoli, 1er
☎ 01 47 03 61 61;
fax 01 42 60 41 78
ℯ www.esprit-de
-france.com/paris/bright
on/esazbri00.htm
Ⓜ Tuileries

Hôtel des Deux Îles

(5, E6) Under the same friendly and helpful management as the Hôtel de Lutèce, the Deux Îles has tiny-but-cheerful, comfortable rooms and a great location on romantic Île St-Louis.

✉ 59 rue St-Louis en l'Île, 4e ☎ 01 43 26 13 35; fax 01 43 29 60 25
Ⓜ Pont Marie

Hôtel Familia (5, E4)

Choose either photogenic street views (including a glimpse of Notre Dame from some top-floor rooms) or a quiet room at the back of this charming Latin Quarter hotel. Some of the 30 rooms may be small but all have bar-fridge and satellite TV.

✉ 11 rue des Écoles, 5e
☎ 01 43 54 55 27;
fax 01 43 29 61 77
ℯ www.hotel-paris
-familia.com
Ⓜ Cardinal Lemoine

Hôtel des Grandes Écoles (5, E4)

Just a *boule* toss from the Place de la Contrescarpe, this popular hotel has one of the loveliest positions in the Quartier Latin. Tucked away in a medieval street, its courtyard garden (James Joyce had rooms here) is the perfect place to sip Pouilly Fumé on a summer evening.

✉ 75 rue du Cardinal
Lemoine, 5e ☎ 01 43 26 79 23; fax 01 43 25 28 15
ℯ hotel.grandes
.ecoles@wanadoo.fr
Ⓜ Cardinal Lemoine

Hôtel des Marronniers

(3, F9) Small, charming and spotless rooms – many with a view of St-Germain des Prés or overlooking the private garden – in the heart of the antique dealers' quarter. Scrumptious breakfasts are served in your room or under the chestnuts (*marroniers*).

✉ 21 rue Jacob, 6e
☎ 01 43 25 30 60;
fax 01 40 46 83 56
Ⓜ St-Germain des Prés

Hôtel Lenox St-Germain (3, F8)

Simple, uncluttered and comfortable rooms upstairs and a late-opening 1930s-style bar downstairs attract a chic clientele.

✉ 9 rue de l'Université, 7e ☎ 01 42 96 10 95; fax 01 42 61 52 83
ℯ www.lenoxsaintger main.com Ⓜ Rue du Bac

Hôtel Saint Christophe (3, J12)

This comfortable little hotel is handy to the nightlife around Place de la Contrescarpe and just a short walk from Notre Dame. The rooms away from busy rue Monge are the quietest.

✉ 17 rue Lacépède, 5e
☎ 01 43 31 81 54;
fax 01 43 31 12 54
ℯ www.charm-hotel
-paris.com
Ⓜ Place Monge

Rob Flynn

MID-RANGE

Grand Hôtel Jeanne d'Arc (5, E8)

This small hotel near lovely Place du Marché Ste-Catherine is a great little *pied-à-terre* for your peregrinations among the museums, bars and restaurants of the Marais, Village St-Paul and Bastille.

✉ 3 rue de Jarente, 4e
☎ 01 48 87 62 11;
fax 01 48 87 37 31
Ⓜ St-Paul

Hôtel des Arts (3, B11)

Cheap and funky hotel with loads of personality (and resident parrot) in a little alley near the Grands Boulevards.

✉ 7 cité Bergère (off rue Bergère), 9e
☎ 01 42 46 73 30;
fax 01 48 00 94 42
Ⓜ Grands Boulevards

Hôtel Chopin (3, B10)

This two-star hotel was built as part of one of Paris' most delightful 19th-century covered shopping arcades. It may be a little faded around the edges,

The home fires burn at Jeanne d'Arc.

Rob Flynn

Serviced Apartments

Staying in a serviced apartment is like staying in a hotel without all the extras, and can be cheaper for families/groups or longer stays (seven days or more). **Citadines Apparthôtels** (☎ 08 25 33 33 32; fax 01 47 59 04 70; Ⓔ www.citadines.com) has 18 properties throughout Paris with studios and apartments catering for 1-6 people.

Flatôtel International (☎ 01 45 75 62 20; fax 01 53 95 20 39; 14 rue du Théâtre, 15e; Ⓜ Charles Michels) has a range of short- and long-term serviced options ranging from studios to executive penthouses with views over the Tour Eiffel and the Seine.

---

but it's still enormously evocative of the *belle époque* and the welcome is always warm. Top floors are most comfortable.

✉ 46 Passage Jouffroy (entry 10 blvd Montmartre), 9e
☎ 01 47 70 58 10;
fax 01 42 47 00 70
Ⓜ Grands Boulevards

Hôtel de L'Espérance (3, K12)

Just a couple of minutes' walk south of lively rue Mouffetard, this quiet, pleasant and immaculately kept hotel is excellent value in a great location.

✉ 15 rue Pascal, 5e
☎ 01 47 07 10 99;
fax 01 43 37 56 19
Ⓜ Censier Daubenton

Hôtel Marignan (5, D4)

The excellent value and free use of a fridge, microwave, washing machine (and dryer) draws a steady stream of long-haulers to this friendly Latin Quartier local.

✉ 13 rue du Sommerard, 5e
☎ 01 43 25 31 03
Ⓔ reservemarignan @wanadoo.fr
Ⓜ Maubert-Mutualité

Hôtel Meridional (3, F15)

Friendly, secure and comfortable (if a touch on the charmless side), conveniently sited just a few minutes' walk from the bright lights of Bastille and on a direct metro line from Gare du Nord. Some top-floor rooms have tiny balconies over the boulevard.

✉ 36 blvd Richard-Lenoir, 11e ☎ 01 48 05 75 00; fax 01 43 57 42 85 Ⓔ www.paris -tourism.com/hotel -meridional Ⓜ Bréguet Sabin, Bastille

Hôtel Michelet-Odéon (5, B3)

Only a minute's walk from the Jardin du Luxembourg, this 42-room hotel has tasteful, generously proportioned rooms, modern bathrooms and lots of satisfied customers. Upper floors have good views over the busy Place de l'Odéon.

✉ 6 Place de l'Odéon, 6e ☎ 01 53 10 05 60; fax 01 46 34 55 35 Ⓔ www.hotel micheletodeon.com Ⓜ Odéon

Hôtel de Nice (5, D7)
This warm, family-run place is right in the thick of things. The welcoming English-speaking owners make you feel right at home; guests have even been known to sunbathe on the balconies.
✉ 42bis rue de Rivoli, 4e ☎ 01 42 78 55 29; fax 01 42 78 36 07
Ⓜ Hôtel de Ville

Hôtel Saint Jacques (5, D4) Audrey Hepburn and Cary Grant, who filmed scenes of *Charade* here, would commend the mod-cons which now complement the original 19th-century detailing (ornamented ceilings, iron staircase) of this adorable little hotel. The evening balcony views of the Panthéon are magic.
✉ 35 rue des Écoles, 5e ☎ 01 44 07 45 45; fax 01 43 25 65 50
ⓔ hotelsaintjacques @wanadoo.fr
Ⓜ Maubert-Mutualité

Nostalgia of the Seventh Art.

Rob Flynn

Hôtel du Septième Art (5, E7) Somewhat reminiscent of a Shinjuku love hotel, this is a fun place for movie buffs – reeking of Hollywood nostalgia and with a black-and-white movie theme throughout, right down to the tiled floors and bathrooms. A cosy place to hang your wig for a couple of days.
✉ 20 rue St-Paul, 4e ☎ 01 44 54 85 00; fax 01 42 77 69 10
ⓔ hotel7art@wanadoo .fr Ⓜ St-Paul

Timhôtel Montmartre (4, C5) It may be a modern chain hotel, but the location is right: on the pretty square where Picasso and his mates changed the course of modern art in the Bateau Lavoir. Some of the rooms on the 4th and 5th floors have stunning views of the city.
✉ 11 Place Émile Goudeau, 18e ☎ 01 42 55 74 79; fax 01 42 55 71 01
ⓔ montmartre@tim hotel.fr Ⓜ Abbesses

Hôtel Tiquetonne (3, K5) If you're looking for good-value digs smack in the middle of party-town, this vintage cheapie may not be all that inspirational but it's clean and comfortable.
✉ 6 rue Tiquetonne, 2e ☎ 01 42 36 94 58; fax 01 42 36 02 94
Ⓜ Étienne Marcel

Airport Hotels

If you're worried about missing your flight, rest easy by staying at one of the following airport hotels:

Roissy Charles de Gaulle
- **Cocoon** (☎ 01 48 62 06 16, fax 01 48 62 56 97) sleep 'cabins' at CDG Terminal 1; 16hrs max.
- **Hilton** (☎ 01 49 19 77 77; fax 01 49 19 77 78; ⓔ cdghitwrm@hilton.com)
- **Ibis** (☎ 01 49 19 19 19, fax 01 49 19 19 21)
- **Novotel** (☎ 01 49 19 27 27; fax 01 49 19 27 99; ⓔ h1014@accor-hotels.com)

Orly
- **Hilton** (☎ 01 45 12 45 12; fax 01 45 12 45 00; ⓔ oryhitwgm@hilton.com)
- **Ibis** (☎ 01 56 70 50 50, fax 01 56 70 50 70)
- **Mercure** (☎ 01 46 87 23 37; fax 01 46 87 71 92; ⓔ h1246@accor-hotels.com)

BUDGET

Auberge Internationale des Jeunes (2, F12)
This clean and very friendly hostel, 700m east of Place de la Bastille, attracts a young, international crowd and is very full in summer. Open 24hrs, but rooms are closed for cleaning 10am-3pm. Book ahead: they'll hold a bed for you if you call from the train station.
✉ **10 rue Trousseau, 11e ☎ 01 47 00 62 00; fax 01 47 00 33 16**
e **www.aijparis.com**
Ⓜ **Ledru Rollin**

Hôtel des Académies
(3, K8) This 21-room hotel located in the former artists' quarter of Montparnasse has been run by the same friendly family since 1920. It retains an authentic 1950s feel, and offers clean, cheap and basic lodgings.
✉ **15 rue de la Grande Chaumière, 6e**
☎ **01 43 26 66 44; fax 01 43 26 03 72**
Ⓜ **Vavin**

Hôtel Castex **(3, G14)**
Barely a minute's stroll from Bastille, this immaculate and welcoming hotel has 27 unpretentious but comfortable (even spacious!) rooms (no TV). It's excellent value – but be prepared for some serious stair-climbing. The loyal clientele know to book well in advance.
✉ **5 rue Castex, 4e**
☎ **01 42 72 31 52; fax 01 42 72 57 91**
e **www.castexhotel .com** Ⓜ **Bastille**

Hôtel Gay Lussac
(5, D2) This family-run, one-star place has a bit of character and small rooms at tiny prices; larger rooms

(with shower) won't cost you much more. It's a few minutes' walk from the Jardin du Luxembourg and Quartier Latin.
✉ **29 rue Gay Lussac, 5e** ☎ **01 43 54 23 96; fax 01 40 51 79 49**
🚆 **RER Luxembourg**

Hôtel de Nevers
(3, D15) Good-value and friendly digs just a short stroll from the Marais and Oberkampf areas.
✉ **53 rue de Malte, 11e**
☎ **01 47 00 56 18; fax 01 43 57 77 39**
e **www.hoteldenevers .com** Ⓜ **République**

MIJE Hostels (5, E7)
If you're between 18-30, one of the best deals in Paris has to be the three popular hostels run by the Maisons Internationales des Jeunes Étudiants, all in converted 17th-century buildings in the Marais. Great digs, great locations and great prices.
✉ **11 rue du Fauconnier, 4e** ☎ **01 42 74 23 45; fax 01 40 27 81 64**
e **www.mije.com**
Ⓜ **St-Paul**

Le Village Hostel
(4, D7) This fine 26-room hostel with beamed ceilings and views of Sacré Cœur has beds in 2-6 person rooms. All rooms have showers and WC; prices include breakfast. There's also a bar, kitchen facilities and a lovely terrace for sitting outside.
✉ **20 rue d'Orsel, 18e**
☎ **01 42 64 22 02; fax 01 42 64 22 04**
e **www.villagehostel.fr**
Ⓜ **Anvers**

Young & Happy Hostel (3, K12)
This clean, friendly, English-speaking hostel, in the happening (and *noisy*) Quartier Latin, is very popular with American and Japanese backpackers. The rooms are closed from 11am-5pm but reception is always open, and the 2am curfew is strictly enforced. There's CNN and MTV in the TV lounge.
✉ **80 rue Mouffetard, 5e** ☎ **01 45 35 09 53; fax 01 47 07 22 24**
e **www.youngandha ppy.fr** Ⓜ **Place Monge**

facts for the visitor

Simon Bracken

ARRIVAL & DEPARTURE

Paris can be reached by direct (and often cut-price) flights from major cities all over the globe. It's within a couple of hours' flying time of major European cities such as London, Barcelona, Amsterdam, Berlin, Vienna, Prague and Rome.

Paris is also at the centre of an intricate network of road and high-speed train routes (just 3hrs to London via the Channel Tunnel!). Wherever you're going, you can get there from Paris.

Air

Two major airports serve Paris, both well connected to the city by train, bus and taxi.

Roissy Charles de Gaulle

Paris' main international airport is 30km northeast of the city centre. There are several terminals, so make sure you know which one your flight leaves from; and leave plenty of time to get your flight, as the airport is large and complex. A free *vedette* (shuttle bus) links the terminals with each other and with the Roissy train station every 5mins.

There are no luggage storage facilities at the airport.

Information

General Inquiries ☎ 01 48 62 22 80
Flight Information ☎ 08 36 68 15 15
  Air France ☎ 08 20 82 08 20
  British Airways ☎ 08 25 82 50 40
  Delta ☎ 08 00 35 40 80
  Qantas ☎ 08 20 82 05 00
  United ☎ 08 10 72 72 72

Airport Access

Train Roissyrail (RER Line B) links the city with the airport (40mins) every 15mins 5.30am–midnight (€7.35). There are two stations at the airport: CDG1 for terminals T1 and T9 (by free shuttle bus) and CDG2 for terminal T2.

Bus Roissybus (☎ 01 48 04 18 24) links the airport with rue Scribe, Place de l'Opéra (45mins), every 15mins 5.45am–11pm (€7.35).

Shuttle Air France shuttle (☎ 01 41 56 89 00) links the airport with Place Charles de Gaulle and Porte Maillot every 20mins 5.45am–11pm (€10/5 one way); Gare de Lyon and Gare de Montparnasse every 30mins 7am–9pm (€12/6 one way).

Parishuttle (☎ 08 00 63 34 40 or 01 43 90 91 91) and Paris Airports Service (☎ 01 55 98 10 808) provide door-to-door service which costs €23 single and €13 for two or more passengers. Pre-booking is required.

Taxi The tariff to central Paris (30-60mins) is €35-50.

Orly

Orly, 18km south of the city centre, has two terminals – Ouest (only domestic flights) and Sud (some international flights). There are no luggage storage facilities at the airport.

Information

General Inquiries & Flight Information
☎ 01 49 75 15 15

Airport Access

Train The Orlyval shuttle train links Orly with RER line B at Antony (7mins), every 7mins 6am-10.30pm, Sun 7am-11pm (€7.10).

Bus Orlybus (☎ 08 36 684 114) links the airport with Place Denfert Rochereau (25mins) every 12mins 6am-11pm (€5.65).

Jetbus (☎ 01 69 01 00 09) links Orly with the Villejuif-Louis Aragon metro stop (15mins) every 15mins 6am-10pm (€4.80).

Shuttle Air France shuttle (☎ 01 41 56 89 00) links the airport with Gare Montparnasse and Aérogare des Invalides (30mins) every 12mins 6am-11pm (€7.65).

Parishuttle (☎ 08 00 63 34 40 or 01 43 90 91 91) and Paris Airports Service (☎ 01 49 62 78 78) provide door-to-door service (both firms: €25 single, €13 two or more people). Pre-booking required.

Taxi The tariff to central Paris (20-30mins) is €25-30.

Bus

Bus travel is rare in France, though Eurolines (**e** www.eurolines.com) has services throughout Europe. Its office (☎ 01 43 54 11 99) is at 55 rue St Jacques, 5e. The international bus terminal (☎ 08 36 69 52 52) is at 28 av du Général de Gaulle, 20e Ⓜ Gallieni.

Train

Paris has six major train stations: Gare d'Austerlitz, Gare de l'Est, Gare de Lyon, Gare du Nord, Gare Montparnasse and Gare St Lazare. Train information is available for TGV and mainline services on ☎ 08 36 35 35 35 and for suburban and RER services on ☎ 08 36 68 77 14; you can also find service info and ticket prices at **e** www.sncf.fr online.

Eurostar

The passenger train service (☎ 08 36 35 35 39; UK ☎ 09 90 186 186; **e** www.eurostar.com) through the Channel Tunnel runs between Paris Gare du Nord and London's Waterloo Station. The trip takes 3hrs station to station with a one-hour time zone change between France and England. The confusing fare structure ranges from UK£60-270 return from London, depending on when you travel.

Travel Documents

Passport
Visitors must carry their passport or European Union (EU) national ID card at all times.

Visa
Visas are not required by citizens of Australia, Canada, the EU, Israel, New Zealand and USA (for visits up to three months). Everyone else requires a 'Schengen Visa' (valid for most of Western Europe). Visas are available through French consulates or on arrival, with an onward ticket.

Return/Onward Ticket
Usually only necessary if you require a Schengen Visa (see Visas above).

Customs

No guns, ammunition, illegal drugs or nuclear waste.

Duty Free

You can no longer buy goods at duty-free prices if travelling only between the member countries of the EU.

The usual import allowances of duty-free goods apply: tobacco (200 cigarettes, 50 cigars or 250g of loose tobacco), alcohol (1L of strong liquor or 2L of less than 22% alcohol by volume; 2L of wine), coffee (500g or 200g of extracts) and perfume (50g of perfume and 250mL of eau de toilette).

Departure Tax

Departure tax is prepaid – it is included in the price of your ticket.

GETTING AROUND

Paris has a fast, efficient and safe (though strike-prone) public transit system operated by RATP (e www.ratp.fr). Wherever you go, you're never more than 500m from a metro station, and even closer to a bus route. In summer the Batobus river taxi plies the Seine between the Tour Eiffel and Notre Dame.

Travel Passes

The **Mobilis** and **Paris Visite** passes allow unlimited travel on the metro, RER and SNCF suburban lines, buses, the Noctambus system, trams and the Montmartre funicular railway. Mobilis (€5-18) allows unlimited travel for one day in two (Paris) or eight (Île de France) zones. Paris Visite passes are valid for one-five consecutive days of travel in either three, five or eight zones (€8.40-54) and include discounts at some museums and shops. Both passes are available at larger metro and RER stations, at SNCF bureaus in Paris and at the airports.

Bus

Buses can be a much better way of seeing the sights while on the move. Services run frequently 7am-8.30pm, but are reduced at night and on Sundays. As your bus approaches, wave the driver down. Any journey that starts and ends within Paris costs one metro ticket – cancel it in the machine onboard. Flash your Mobilis or Paris Visite pass at the driver.

Noctambus

The Noctambus (☎ 08 36 68 41 14) network operates after the metro has closed for the night. Buses, marked with a black owl in front of a yellow moon, depart every hour on the half-hour 1-5.30am from just west of the Hôtel de Ville and the service's 18 lines cover most of the city. Tickets cost €2.45 and Mobilis or Paris Visite passes are valid.

Train

Paris' underground network is simple to use and is usually the fastest way of getting around the city. It consists of two separate but linked systems: the Métropolitain, known as the *métro*, which has 14 lines and over 300 stations; and the RER, a network of five suburban services that pass through the city centre. Normally, you'd only use the RER if you wanted to cover large distances quickly, eg St-Michel to Tour Eiffel. Free metro/RER maps are available at metro ticket windows.

The metro operates approximately 5.30am-12.30am; trains run every 5mins or so. Each line is designated by a number, a colour and a *direction*, or final destination, which ensures you're on the right platform.

For metro, RER and bus system information, call RATP's 24hr lines ☎ 08 36 68 77 14 (French) or ☎ 08 36 68 41 14 (English); online, check e www.ratp.fr for details.

Information on SNCF's suburban services (including some RER lines) is available on ☎ 08 36 35 35 35, ☎ 08 36 67 68 69 (recording) or at e www.sncf.fr.

Tickets

Tickets for travel within the Paris city limits on the metro and RER network cost €1.30 if bought individually (*ticket*) and €9.30 for a *carnet* of 10. Children under 4 travel free; children under 10 half-fare. Tickets are sold at windows and machines at every metro station, though not always at each and every entrance.

Carry your ticket with you until you have exited the station as spot checks (and spot fines) are frequent.

Taxi

Parisian taxi drivers have a reputation for arrogance but, within reason, it's all part of the fun.

Radio-dispatched 24hr companies include: Taxis Bleus (English-speaking operators ☎ 01 49 36 10 10), G7 Radio (☎ 01 47 39 01 47; English ☎ 01 41 27 66 99; airport travel ☎ 01 41 27 66 66), Alpha Taxis (☎ 01 45 85 85 85), and Artaxi (☎ 01 42 03 50 50).

Fares & Charges

The *prise en charge* (flag-fall fee) is around €2. Within the city, it costs €0.55/km for travel Mon-Sat, 7am-7pm. At night, on Sundays and holidays it's €0.90/km. It costs €20/hr to have a taxi wait for you.

There's an extra €1.55 surcharge for a 4th passenger – ask permission first. Each bag over 5kg costs €1 and from certain train stations there's a €1 supplement. The usual tip is just a euro or two no matter what the fare. Make reservations for peak-hour and airport travel.

Approximate Fares

Notre Dame–Jardin du Luxembourg €4.50
Notre Dame–Musée d'Orsay €5
Châtelet–Bastille €6.50
Gare du Nord–Châtelet €8
Hôtel de Ville–Arc de Triomphe €10
Sacré Cœur/Bastille–Tour Eiffel €10/12

Car & Motorcycle

Driving in Paris is difficult but not impossible (except for the nervy, faint-hearted or indecisive). The fastest way across town is via the *périphérique* (ring road) or the *quais* (left bank goes west; the right, east).

You'll mostly pay €1.50 to park your car on the street – look for white-outlined spaces marked *payant*; yellow markings mean no parking. Large municipal parking garages charge around €2-3/hr or, for periods of 12 to 24hrs, €12-20. Parking fines are usually €12 or €30.

Road Rules

Vehicles drive on the right-hand side of the road; seat belts are compulsory (front and back); and motorcyclists must wear helmets. The minimum driving age is 18.

Vehicles on your right always have priority, even on major roads and in roundabouts.

Speed Limits 50km/h in built-up areas, 90km/h on undivided highways, 110km/h on dual carriageways and 130km/h on autoroutes.

The blood-alcohol limit of 0.05% is enforced with random breath checks and severe punishments.

Car Rental

Major companies – Avis (☎ 08 02 05 05 05), Europcar (☎ 08 03 35 23 52) and Hertz (☎ 01 39 38 38 38) – have offices in the city and Roissy airport. ADA (☎ 08 36 68 40 02) and Rent A Car 7 (☎ 08 36 69 46 95) are smaller companies. The minimum age to rent a car is 25. Book well ahead if you want to hire an automatic, as most rental cars are manual.

Driving Licence & Permit

Visitors can drive normal vehicles using their home-country driving licence. Some rental companies may demand an International Driving Permit (IDP) too.

Motoring Organisations

The Automobile Club de l'Île de France (☎ 01 40 55 43 00 e acif@ autoclubs-associes.tm.fr), 14 av de la Grande Armée, 17e, sells insurance coverage and can provide basic maps and itinerary suggestions.

PRACTICAL INFORMATION

Climate & When to Go

Just go! Paris is worth visiting at any time of the year (April-May & Sept are best) – though the weather is often unpredictable. Paris' average yearly temperature is 3-12°C (37-53°F) in Jan, 19°C (66°F) in July – but the mercury sometimes drops below zero in winter and can climb to 35°C (95°F) or higher in the middle of summer. Most residents flee the city and many businesses close in Aug.

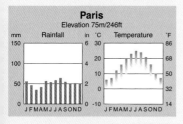

Tourist Information

Tourist Information Abroad

French government tourist offices (usually called Maisons de la France) can provide all sorts of tourist information on Paris, as well as the rest of the country, most of it in the form of brochures. The web address is at [e] www.franceguide.com and their offices include the following:

Australia
    25 Bligh St, Sydney, NSW 2000 ([☎] 02-9231 5244; fax 02-9221 8682; [e] france@bigpond.net.au)

Canada
    1981 McGill College Ave, Suite 490, Montreal, Que H3A 2W9 ([☎] 514-876 9881; fax 514-845 4868; [e] mfrance@attcanada.net)

South Africa
    Oxford Manor, 1st floor, 196 Oxford Rd, Illovo 2196 ([☎] 011-880 8062; fax 011-770 16 66; [e] mdfsa@frenchdoor.co.za)

UK
    178 Piccadilly, London W1J 9AL ([☎] 09068 244 123; fax (0)20-7493 6594; [e] info@mdlf.co.uk)

USA
    444 Madison Ave, 16th fl, New York, NY 10022-6903 ([☎] 410-286-8310; fax 212-838 7855; [e] info@francetourism.com)

Local Tourist Information

The helpful main tourist office ([☎] 08 36 68 31 12) is located at 127 av des Champs Élysées, 8e (3, B3). It is open for business 9am-8pm daily, except Sunday in winter (11am-6pm only).

There are tourist office annexes in the Gare du Nord (2, C10) and the Gare de Lyon (2, G12) open daily, except Sunday and holidays, 8am-8pm. The annexe at the base of the Tour Eiffel (3, F2) is open from May-Sept daily (including holidays) 11am-6pm.

Embassies

Australia
    4 rue Jean Rey, 15e (3, F2; [☎] 01 40 59 33 00; [Ⓜ] Bir Hakeim)

Canada
    35 ave Montaigne, 8e (3, C4; [☎] 01 44 43 29 00; [Ⓜ] Alma Marceau)

New Zealand
    7-ter rue Léonard de Vinci, 16e (3, B1; [☎] 01 45 01 43 43; [Ⓜ] Victor Hugo)

South Africa
    59 Quai d'Orsay, 7e (3, E6; [☎] 01 53 59 23 23; [Ⓜ] Invalides)

UK
    16 rue d'Anjou, 8e (3, C7; [☎] 01 44 51 31 00, emergency 24hrs [☎] 01 42 66 29 79; [Ⓜ] Concorde)

USA
    2 rue St-Florentin, 1er (3, C7; [☎] 08 36 70 14 88, emergency 24hrs [☎] 01 43 12 49 48; [Ⓜ] Concorde)

Money

Currency

Since 18 February 2002 the sole legal tender in France has been the euro (€), which is divided into 100 cents. Coins come in €1 and €2, and 1, 2, 5, 10, 20 and 50 cents. Notes come in denominations of €5, €10, €20, €50, €100, €200 and a whopping €500.

All euro currency is legal tender in the 11-nation euro zone. Euro coins have national motifs, but have the same value throughout the zone and any can be spent in France. Euro notes have no national motifs.

France's former currency, the French franc (FF) will continue to be convertible at banks until 30 June 2002 at a rate of 6.55957FF to €1. After that date (and for several years to come), you will still be able to convert francs to euros at the Trésor Public or Banque de France at the same fixed rate. You may find old FF prices referred to in the next few years.

This book was researched during the transition period, and some prices may undergo further change as the euro comes into use. For further information visit the European Union's website at **e** www.europa .eu.int/euro/html/entry.html or the French Government's site at **e** www.euro.gouv.fr.

Travellers Cheques

Travellers cheques are not widely accepted in France – post offices and exchange bureaus are your best bets. At the time of writing there was little experience of travellers cheques in euro denominations, so $US remain the safest bet. American Express (3, B8; ☎ 01 47 77 70 00), 14 rue Scribe, 9e, does not charge a commission on its own travellers cheques.

Credit Cards

Visa is the most widely accepted credit card, followed by Master-Card. American Express and Diners Club cards are only accepted at upmarket establishments. For lost cards contact:

American Express	☎ 01 47 77 70 00
Diners Club	☎ 01 49 06 17 50
MasterCard	☎ 08 00 90 11 79
Visa	☎ 08 00 90 20 33

ATMs

Most ATMs in Paris are linked to the Cirrus and/or Maestro networks, so obtaining cash is usually not a problem if your card uses one of these services: check this before you leave home. Ensure you know your PIN number. Some ATMs may accept PINs with four digits only; if you have a problem, try another bank. You should also check (and probably raise) your daily withdrawal limit before you leave home.

Euro – FF Conversion
(to the nearest franc)

€	FF	€	FF
1	7	20	131
2	13	25	164
3	20	30	197
4	26	40	262
5	33	50	328
6	40	60	394
7	46	70	460
8	53	80	525
9	59	90	590
10	66	100	656
11	72	200	1312
12	79	300	1968
13	85	400	2624
14	92	500	3280
15	98	1,000	6560

Changing Money

Foreign cash is not the best way to carry money in France; it's far better to bring euros with you if you can. Banks and exchange bureaus often give poorer rates for cash than travellers cheques.

Major train stations and hotels have exchange facilities which operate evenings, weekends and holidays. Banque de France offers the best exchange rates, but it does not accept Eurocheques or provide credit-card cash advances. Many post offices perform exchange transactions for a middling rate.

Tipping

French law requires that restaurant, cafe and hotel bills include a mandatory service charge of 15%, so a *pourboire* (tip) is neither necessary nor expected in most cases. However, most people leave a few euros in restaurants, unless the service was bad. They rarely tip in cafes and bars when they've just had a coffee or a drink.

Discounts

Concessions (usually 30-50%) abound for youth, students and seniors on everything from transport to museums. Bring whatever concession ID you have from home and flash it every time you pull out your wallet.

Student & Youth Cards

The International Student Identity Card (ISIC) is widely accepted throughout France and affords half-price admissions, discounted air and ferry tickets, and cheap meals in student cafeterias. Many places stipulate a maximum age, usually 24 or 25.

Seniors' Cards

Reduced-entry prices are charged for people over 60 at most cultural centres, including museums, galleries and public theatres. SNCF issues the Carte Senior to those over 60, with reductions of 20-50% on train tickets.

Travel Insurance

A policy covering theft, loss, medical expenses and compensation for cancellation or delays in your travel arrangements is highly recommended. If items are lost or stolen, make sure you get a police report straight away – otherwise your insurer might not pay up.

Opening Hours

Opening hours for shops, banks, museums and restaurants can seem unpredictable in Paris. Many places are closed on Sun and either Mon or Tues, and many also close for lunch (usually 12.30-2.30pm). Many restaurants close before 11pm; on the other hand, many museums have *nocturnes* or late opening hours at least one night per week.

Banks
  Mon-Fri 9am-4.30pm and some branches Sat morning; some close for lunch.

Pharmacies
  Mon-Sat 9am-6pm

Post Offices
  Mon-Fri 8am-7pm, Sat 8am-noon

Shops
  Mon-Sat 9/10am-6.30/7pm; some open Sun mornings Jul-Aug and to 10pm once a week.

Tourist Sites
  Hours vary widely, but 9am-5.30pm is standard for smaller attractions; most museums close Mon or Tues and some on public holidays.

Public Holidays

Jan 1	New Year's Day (Jour de l'An)
Mar/Apr	Easter Sunday (Pâques)
Mar/Apr	Easter Monday (Lundi de Pâques)
May 1	May Day (Fête de Travail)
May 8	Victory in Europe Day (Victorie 1945)
May	Ascension Thursday (L'Ascension)
May/June	Whit Sunday/Whit Monday (Pentecôte/Lundi de Pentecôte)
July 14	Bastille Day (Fête Nationale)
Aug 15	Assumption Day (L'Assomption)
Nov 1	All Saints' Day (La Toussaint)
Nov 11	Armistice Day (Le onze Novembre)
Dec 24	Christmas Day (Noël)

Time

France is 1hr ahead of GMT/UTC. During daylight-saving periods it is 2hrs ahead. In standard time, at noon in Paris it's:

11am in London
6am in New York
3am in Los Angeles
noon in Johannesburg
9pm in Sydney
11pm in Auckland

Electricity

Voltage is 220V AC, 50Hz. Plugs have two or three round pins; adapters are best brought from home but can be bought at FNAC in Les Halles and BHV. US appliances will fry in Paris without an adapter.

Weights & Measures

France invented and still uses the metric system – though it's still possible to order by the *livre* (pound, 500g). See the conversion table on page 122 for more.

Post

La Poste (☎ 08 01 63 02 01) runs the country's mail system. The main post office (☎ 01 40 28 20 00) at 52 rue du Louvre, 1er (3, D11), is five blocks north of the north-eastern corner of the Louvre and is open 24hrs for mail services.

Each *arrondissement* has a five-digit postcode, beginning with 750 and ending with the *arrondissement* number, so 75001 for the 1er, 75019 for the 19e. The 16e has two postcodes: 75016 and 75116.

Postal Rates

Stamps are sold at post office counters and at some *tabacs* (tobacconists). Domestic letters (up to 20g) and postcards and letters cost €0.46 within the EU, €0.67 to the US and Canada, and €0.79 to Australasia.

Opening Hours

Post offices are open Mon-Fri 8am-7pm, Sat 8am-noon; the main post office is open 24hrs.

Telephone

French telephone numbers generally have 10 digits, the first two being the area code. Dial all 10 digits for calls within France; drop the initial zero when calling from outside France. Telephone booths are common throughout Paris and accept coins, credit cards and phonecards.

Phonecards

Most public telephones require a phonecard *(télécarte)* which can be purchased at post offices, *tabacs*, supermarket checkout counters, SNCF ticket windows, Paris metro stations and anywhere you see a blue sticker reading *télécarte en vente ici*. Cards worth 50 calling units cost €7.50; those worth 120 units are €14.85.

Lonely Planet's eKno Communication Card (ⓔ www.ekno .com), specifically designed for travellers, provides competitive international calls (avoid using it for local calls), messaging services and free email. The toll-free eKno number to call when you are in France is ☎ 08 00 90 08 50.

Mobile Phones

France uses the GSM 900/1800 cellular phone system, compatible with phones sold in the UK, Australia and most of Asia, but not those from North America or Japan. To use your cell phone in France, ensure you request 'international roaming' from your telecommunications company before you leave home.

Country & City Codes

France	☎ 33
Paris region	☎ 01
Northwest France	☎ 02
Northeast France	☎ 03
Southeast France & Corsica	☎ 04
Southwest France	☎ 05

Useful Numbers

Operator/Directory Inquiries	☎ 12
International Directory Inquiries	☎ 00 33 12

+ international dialling code of the country (use 11 in place of 1 for US and Canada)

International Operator	☎ 00 33

+ international dialling code of country

International Direct Dial Codes

Dial ☎ 00+:

Australia	☎ 61
Canada	☎ 1
Japan	☎ 81
New Zealand	☎ 64
South Africa	☎ 27
UK	☎ 44
USA	☎ 1

Digital Resources

To get your email fix or browse the web, drop into one of the many cybercafes mushrooming around town or at most La Poste branchés.

Internet Service Providers

The local access number for AOL is ☎ 01 40 64 16 70, for Compuserve ☎ 01 41 02 03 04, and for AT&T Global Network ☎ 08 60 07 60 01. The most popular local access providers are Wanadoo (ⓔ www .wandoo.fr, ☎ 08 01 10 51 05) and Club Internet (ⓔ www.club-inter net.fr, ☎ 08 01 80 09 00).

Internet Cafes

Cyber Cube
☎ 01 53 10 30 50; ⓔ www.cybercube .fr; 3 rue Molière, 1er (3, D9) Ⓜ Pyramides & 5 rue Mignon, 6e (5, B4) Ⓜ Odéon ◷ 10am-10pm, except Sun ⓢ €0.15/min

easyEverything
☎ 01 42 44 15 15; 37 blvd de Sébastopol, 1er (5, A7) Ⓜ Châtelet-Les Halles & 6 rue de la Harpe, 5e (5, C4) Ⓜ Saint Michel ⓔ www.easyeverything.com/france ◷ 24hrs ⓢ variable pricing from €1.50

Web Bar
☎ 01 42 72 66 55; 32 rue de Picardie, 3e (5, C9) Ⓜ Filles du Calvaire, Temple ⓔ www.webbar.fr ◷ 8.30am-2am ⓢ €3/hr or subscription

Useful Sites

For information and links to useful travel resources start at Lonely Planet's websites (ⓔ www.lonely planet.com for information in English and ⓔ www.lonelyplanet.fr in French). You could also try:

The Paris Pages
ⓔ www.paris.org

Paris Tourist office
ⓔ www.paris-touristoffice.com

Think Paris
ⓔ www.thinkparis.com

Doing Business

Le Monde , Le Figaro and Les Echos are the best print news sources for business and finance.

Many hotels provide business facilities, including conference rooms, secretarial services, fax and photocopying services, use of computers and private office space. Some also provide specialist translation services. Or try NewWorks (☎ 01 72 74 24 00 e www.new works.net) with three central serviced bureaux.

The business centre (☎ 01 48 62 22 90, fax 01 48 62 61 29) inside terminal 1 of Roissy Charles de Gaulle airport has catered meeting rooms, offices and business equipment.

Newspapers & Magazines

Paris' main daily newspapers are Le Monde, Liberation and Le Figaro. The most popular magazines are L'Express, Le Point and Le Nouvel Observateur.

English-language newspapers widely available in Paris are the International Herald Tribune, European, The Times, Guardian, USA Today, Financial Times, Newsweek, Time and the Economist. For English-language entertainment listings, there's a 'Time Out' supplement in the weekly Pariscope.

Radio

The Radio France network offers four high-quality services in French: France Inter (opinion & music 87.8FM), France Info (news & views 105.5FM), France Culture (talk 93.5/93.9FM) and France Musiques (91.7/92.1FM). For music, try Radio Nova (hip 101.5FM), Cherie FM (mainstream 91.3FM) or NRJ (rock/pop 100.3FM).

BBC World Service/BBC for Europe (news & views 648AM), Voice of America (1197AM), Radio France Internationale (English noon, 2 & 4pm 738AM).

TV

There are five free-to-air channels – three state-owned (France 2, F3 and Arte/La Cinquième) and two commercial (TF1 & M6). In addition there is a subscription movie channel, Canal+, plus a range of cable and satellite offerings, with programming from CNN and the BBC amongst others.

The main news bulletin is at 8pm on TF1 and France 2, and 8.30pm on Arte. Programming on the free-to-air stations is entirely in French, though there's the odd movie or serial in English with French subtitles.

Many cable-equipped hotels offer CNN and BBC news channels. While the majority of English-language programs are dubbed into French for the local audience, films and series are often shown in English (look for the letters 'vo' – version originale), with French subtitles.

Photography & Video

Print and slide film are both widely available.

Photography is rarely forbidden, except in certain museums and art galleries, though in some areas police may move you along if you set up a tripod.

France uses the PAL (Phase Alternative Line) video system, which isn't compatible with other standards unless converted.

Health

Immunisations

Immunisations are required only if you've visited an infected country in the preceding 14 days (aircraft refuelling stops not included).

Precautions

Paris' tap water is perfectly safe to drink, although it does have quite a strong chlorine taste. Many French cheeses and some meat products (eg *rillettes)* are unpasteurised and may cause some people stomach upsets.

Insurance & Medical Treatment

Travel insurance is advisable to cover any medical treatment you may need while in Paris. EU residents are covered for emergency medical treatment throughout the EU. The coverage provided by most private US health insurance policies continues if you travel abroad, at least for a limited period.

Canadians covered by the Régie de l'Assurance-Maladie du Québec can benefit from certain reimbursement agreements with France's national health-care system.

Medical Services

There are some 50 *assistance publique* (public health service) hospitals in Paris. If you need an ambulance urgently, call ☎ 15 or ☎ 01 40 38 07 33. For emergency treatment, call Urgences Médicales on ☎ 01 48 28 40 04 or SOS Médecins on ☎ 01 47 07 77 77. Both offer 24hr house calls. If you can travel, some possibilities are:

Hôpital Américain (2, B4)
   ☎ 01 46 41 25 25; 63 blvd Victor Hugo, 17e Ⓜ Porte Maillot

Hôpital Franco-Britannique (2, B4)
   ☎ 01 46 39 22 22; 3 rue Barbès, 17e Ⓜ Anatole-France

Hôtel Dieu (5, C5)
   ☎ 01 42 34 81 31; Place du Parvis Notre Dame, 4e Ⓜ Cité

Dental Services

La Pitié-Salpêtrière (☎ 01 42 16 00 00), rue Bruand, 13e (2, H11), is the only dental hospital with extended hours. The after-hours entrance (open 5.30pm-8.30am) is at 47 blvd de l'Hôpital.

SOS Dentaire (☎ 01 47 07 33 68), 87 blvd de Port Royal, 13e (2, H9), is a private dentists' office open when most dentists are off duty: Mon-Fri 8am-11.45pm, weekends and holidays 9am-12.10pm, 2.20-7.10pm and 8-11.40pm.

Pharmacies

There's a pharmacy on nearly every corner of Paris – look for the green neon crosses. Some chemists with longer opening hours are:

Dérhy/Pharmacie des Champs
   84 av des Champs Élysées, 8e (3, B4) ☎ 01 45 62 02 41; open 24hrs

Dérhy/Pharmacie des Halles
   10 blvd de Sébastopol, 4e (5, B6) ☎ 01 42 72 03 23; open 9am-midnight (from noon Sun & holidays)

Pharmacie Européenne de la Place de Clichy
   6 Place de Clichy, 17e (4, E1); ☎ 01 48 74 65 18; open 24hrs

Toilets

Public toilets are signposted as *toilettes* or WC. Paris' coin-operated public toilets are cheap, clean and plentiful. Open from early morning to 10pm, you get 15mins of heated luxury for just €0.30, and the entire unit is cleaned and disinfected after each use (no need to flush). Children under 10 should be accompanied by an adult, and people with disabilities may need assistance.

Safety Concerns

In general, Paris is a safe city and occurrences of random street assaults are rare. Nonviolent crime (such as pickpocketing and thefts from handbags or packs) is a problem wherever there are crowds, especially around Montmartre, Pigalle, the areas around Forum des Halles and the Centre Pompidou, on the metro at rush hour and the RER line to/from Roissy airport. Be wary of kids who jostle up against you in a crowd or someone carrying a coat to hide their hand.

Metro stations which are probably best avoided late at night include Châtelet-Les Halles (with its seemingly endless corridors), Château Rouge in Montmartre, Gare du Nord, Strasbourg St-Denis, Réaumur Sébastopol and Montparnasse Bienvenüe. Bornes d'alarme (alarm boxes) are located in the centre of each metro/RER platform and in some station corridors.

Lost Property

All lost objects found anywhere in Paris – except those discovered on trains or in train stations – are eventually brought to the city's Bureau des Objets Trouvés (Lost Property Office), 36 rue des Morillons, 15e (2, H6; ☎ 01 55 76 20 20), run by the Préfecture de Police. The lost property office is open Mon, Wed & Fri 8.30am-5pm, Tues & Thurs 8.30am-8pm (to 5pm July-Aug).

Keeping Copies

Keep photocopies of important documents with you, separate from the originals, and leave a copy at home. You can also store details of documents in Lonely Planet's free online Travel Vault, password-protected and accessible worldwide (e www.ekno.lonelyplanet.com).

Emergency Numbers

Ambulance	☎ 15
Police	☎ 17
Police (non-emergency)	☎ 01 55 26 20 00
Fire Brigade	☎ 18
Rape Crisis Hotline	☎ 08 00 05 95 95

Women Travellers

Paris is generally a safe city, and women travelling alone rarely attract unwanted attention. Of course, you should take the normal big-city precautions at night, especially leaving bars and clubs. If you do experience unacceptable behaviour, 'Laissez-moi tranquille!' is a firm but relatively polite way of saying 'Leave me alone!'

The women-only Maison des Femmes, 163 rue de Charenton, 12e (2, G12; ☎ 01 43 43 41 13), is a meeting place for women of all ages and nationalities (open Wed & Fri-Sat 4-7pm; cafe Fri 7-10pm).

The contraceptive pill is available on prescription only, so a visit to the doctor is necessary. Tampons are available from chemists and supermarkets. Condoms are available from pharmacies, and inside some metro stations.

Gay & Lesbian Travellers

France is one of Europe's most liberal countries when it comes to homosexuality, though the lesbian scene is much less public than its gay male counterpart and is centred mainly around women's cafes and bars.

Information & Organisations

The best listing of gay clubs, bars and associations is in the weekly e.m@le, which is free at gay venues or for €1 at newsagents. Others with fewer listings include Tétu, Attitude and Gus. Lesbian publications include Lesbia (monthly, €4) and *Les Nanas* (bimonthly, free). The website e www.citegay.com is useful.

Most of France's major gay organisations are based in Paris and include the following:

ActUp Paris
45 rue Sedaine, 11e (2, F12); ☎ 01 48 06 13 89; e www.actupp.org; Ⓜ Voltaire

Association des Médecins Gais
☎ 01 48 05 81 71; Wed 6-8pm, Sat 2-4pm

Centre Gai et Lesbien (CGL)
3 rue Keller, 11e (2, F12); ☎ 01 43 57 21 47; Ⓜ Ledru Rollin

Écoute Gaie
☎ 01 44 93 01 02; hotline Mon-Fri 6-10pm, Sat 6-8pm

Senior Travellers

Senior citizens are entitled to discounts in France on things like public transport, museum admission fees etc, provided they show proof of age. In some cases a special pass is needed. See Discounts p. 114.

Disabled Travellers

France is not particularly well equipped for the *handicapés* (disabled): kerb ramps are few and far between, older public facilities and bottom-end hotels often lack lifts, and the Paris métro, most of it built decades ago, is hopeless. But physically challenged people who would like to visit Paris can overcome these problems. Most hotels with two or more stars are equipped with lifts, and Michelin's *Guide Rouge* indicates hotels with lifts and facilities for disabled people.

Information & Organisations

In recent years the SNCF has made efforts to make its trains more accessible to people with physical disabilities. Details are available in SNCF's booklet *Guide du Voyageur à Mobilité Réduite*. You can also contact SNCF Accessibilité on ☎ 08 00 15 47 53 (toll-free).

In some places vehicles outfitted for people in wheelchairs provide transport within the city. Details are available from the Groupement pour l'Insertion des Personnes Handicapées Physiques, 98 rue de la Porte Jaune, 92210 Saint Cloud (☎ 01 41 83 15 15).

Access in Paris provides a good overview of facilities available to disabled travellers in Paris; published by RADAR, 12 City Forum, 250 City Rd, London EC1V 8AF (UK ☎ +44 (0)20-7250 3222).

Paris Pratique is available from the Paris tourist office (☎ 08 00 03 37 37) for €10.

Language

Parisians are well used to English-speaking visitors and will usually respond in kind to a polite request. Begin with whatever French you can muster, even if it's *Excusez-moi, madame/monsieur, parlez-vous anglais?* ('Excuse me, madam/sir, do you speak English?')

For more useful words and phrases, see Lonely Planet's *French phrasebook*.

Basics

Yes.	*Oui.*
No.	*Non.*
Maybe.	*Peut-être.*
Please.	*S'il vous plaît.*
Thank you.	*Merci.*
You're welcome.	*Je vous en prie.*
Excuse me.	*Excusez-moi.*
Sorry/Forgive me.	*Pardon.*
Hello/Good morning.	*Bonjour.*
Good evening/ night/bye.	*Bonsoir/Bonne nuit/Au revoir.*
How are you?	*Comment allez-vous? (pol); Comment vas-tu?/ Ça va? (inf)*

Fine, thanks.	*Bien, merci.*
My name is ...	*Je m'appelle ...*
I'm pleased to meet you.	*Enchanté/e (m)/(f)*
I understand.	*Je comprends.*
I don't understand.	*Je ne comprends pas.*
Do you speak English?	*Parlez-vous anglais?*
Could you please write it down?	*Est-ce que vous pouvez l'écrire?*
How much is it?	*C'est combien?*

Getting Around

I want to go to ...	*Je voudrais aller à ...*
What time does the ... leave/arrive?	*À quelle heure part/arrive ...?*
bus (city)	*l'autobus*
ferry	*le ferry(-boat)*
train	*le train*
Where is (the) ...?	*Où est ...?*
bus stop	*l'arrêt d'autobus*
train station	*la gare*
I'd like a ... ticket.	*Je voudrais un billet ...*
one-way/return	*aller-simple/ aller-retour*
How long does the trip take?	*Combien de temps dure le trajet?*
left-luggage locker	*consigne automatique*
platform	*quai*
timetable	*horaire*
I'm looking for ...	*Je cherche ...*
my hotel	*mon hôtel*
the market/ supermarket	*le marché/ supermarché*
a public phone	*une cabine téléphonique*
What time does it open/close?	*Quelle est l'heure d'ouverture/ de fermeture?*
Where is the toilet?	*Où se trouve les toilettes?*
I'd like to make a telephone call.	*Je voudrais téléphoner.*
How do I get to ...?	*Pour aller à ...?*
Is it near/far?	*Est-ce près/loin?*
Go straight ahead.	*Continuez tout droit.*
Turn left/right	*Tournez à gauche/droite.*
behind/in front of	*derrière/devant*

Signs

Entrée/Sortie	*Entrance/Exit*
Ouvert/Fermé	*Open/Closed*
Renseignements	*Information*
Interdit	*Prohibited*
Toilettes, WC	*Toilets*
Hommes/Femmes	*Men/Women*

Time & Dates

What time is it?	*Quelle heure est-il?*
It's (two) o'clock.	*Il est (deux) heures.*
When?	*Quand?*
today/tomorrow/ yesterday	*aujourd'hui/demain/ hier*
morning/ afternoon/ evening	*le matin/ l'après-midi/ le soir*
Monday	*lundi*
Tuesday	*mardi*
Wednesday	*mercredi*
Thursday	*jeudi*
Friday	*vendredi*
Saturday	*samedi*
Sunday	*dimanche*

Numbers

1	*un*
2	*deux*
3	*trois*
4	*quatre*
5	*cinq*
6	*six*
7	*sept*
8	*huit*
9	*neuf*
10	*dix*
15	*quinze*
20	*vingt*
100	*cent*
1000	*mille*

Emergencies

Help!	*Au secours!*
Call a doctor!	*Appelez un médecin!*
Call the police!	*Appelez la police!*
Leave me alone!	*Fichez-moi la paix!*
I'm lost.	*Je me suis égaré /e. (m/f)*

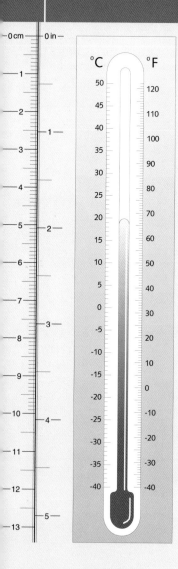

Conversion Table

Clothing Sizes
Measurements approximate only; try before you buy.

Women's Clothing

Aust/NZ	8	10	12	14	16	18
Europe	36	38	40	42	44	46
Japan	5	7	9	11	13	15
UK	8	10	12	14	16	18
USA	6	8	10	12	14	16

Women's Shoes

Aust/NZ	5	6	7	8	9	10
Europe	35	36	37	38	39	40
France only	35	36	38	39	40	42
Japan	22	23	24	25	26	27
UK	3½	4½	5½	6½	7½	8½
USA	5	6	7	8	9	10

Men's Clothing

Aust/NZ	92	96	100	104	108	112
Europe	46	48	50	52	54	56
Japan	S		M	M		L
UK	35	36	37	38	39	40
USA	35	36	37	38	39	40

Men's Shirts (Collar Sizes)

Aust/NZ	38	39	40	41	42	43
Europe	38	39	40	41	42	43
Japan	38	39	40	41	42	43
UK	15	15½	16	16½	17	17½
USA	15	15½	16	16½	17	17½

Men's Shoes

Aust/NZ	7	8	9	10	11	12
Europe	41	42	43	44½	46	47
Japan	26	27	27.5	28	29	30
UK	7	8	9	10	11	12
USA	7½	8½	9½	10½	11½	12½

Weights & Measures

Weight
1kg = 2.2lb
1lb = 0.45kg
1g = 0.04oz
1oz = 28g

Volume
1 litre = 0.26 US gallons
1 US gallon = 3.8 litres
1 litre = 0.22 imperial gallons
1 imperial gallon = 4.55 litres

Length & Distance
1 inch = 2.54cm
1cm = 0.39 inches
1m = 3.3ft = 1.1yds
1ft = 0.3m
1km = 0.62 miles
1 mile = 1.6km

lonely planet

Lonely Planet is the world's most successful independent travel information company with offices in Australia, the US, UK and France. With a reputation for comprehensive, reliable travel information, Lonely Planet is a print and electronic publishing leader, with over 650 titles and 22 series catering for travellers' individual needs.

At Lonely Planet we believe that travellers can make a positive contribution to the countries they visit – if they respect their host communities and spend their money wisely. Since 1986 a percentage of the income from books has been donated to aid and human rights projects.

www.lonelyplanet.com

For news, views and free subscriptions to print and email newsletters, and a full list of Lonely Planet titles, click on our award-winning website.

On the Town

A romantic escape to Paris or a mad shopping dash through New York City, the locals' secret bars or a city's top attractions – whether you have 24 hours to kill or months to explore, Lonely Planet's On the Town products will give you the low-down.

Condensed guides are ideal pocket guides for when time is tight. Their quick-view maps, full-colour layout and opinionated reviews help short-term visitors target the top sights and discover the very best eating, shopping and entertainment options a city has to offer.

For more indepth coverage, **City guides** offer insights into a city's character and cultural background as well as providing broad coverage of where to eat, stay and play. **CitySync**, a digital guide for your handheld unit, allows you to reference stacks of opinionated, well-researched travel information. Portable and durable **City Maps** are perfect for locating those back-street bars or hard-to-find local haunts.

'Ideal for a generation of fast movers.'

– *Gourmet Traveller* on Condensed guides

Condensed Guides

- Amsterdam
- Athens (May 2002)
- Barcelona (May 2002)
- Boston
- California
- Chicago

- Crete
- Dublin
- Frankfurt
- Hong Kong
- London
- New York City
- Paris

- Prague (May 2002)
- Rome
- Sydney
- Tokyo
- Venice (June 2002)
- Washington, DC (May 2002)

index

See also separate indexes for Places to Eat (p. 126), Places to Stay (p. 127), Shops (p. 127) and Sights with map references (p. 128).

PLACES TO EAT

PLACES TO STAY

SHOPS

sights – quick index